AND THEN WE ALL GET TO SHINE

Jody Pignolet

The GREATEST gift you have to give yourself
and the world is your AUTHENTIC SELF.
Find it, connect with it and LIVE from it

And Then We All Get to Shine
By Jody Pignolet

Copyright © 2024 Jody Pignolet

All rights reserved. No part of this publication may be reproduced, distributed, or transmitted in any form or by any means, including photocopying, recording, or other electronic or mechanical methods, without prior written permission of the publisher, except in the case of brief quotations embodied in critical reviews and certain other noncommercial uses permitted by copyright law.

Cover design: Jody Pignolet
About Author photo: Woods Wheatcroft

Jody Pignolet

Table of Contents

THE IDEA	11
INTRODUCTION	13
AU-THEN-TIC-I-TY:	16
the quality of being real or true:	16
WHAT I WANT YOU TO KNOW	20
WHAT ELSE?	25
SECTION I: Your Amazing Self	37
SECTION II - Part 1: Getting to the Real You	45
SECTION II – Part 2: The False You	71
SECTION III: Your Best Self	88
SECTION IV: Making it Yours	98
SECTION V: Doing the Math	132
CONCLUSION	139
APPENDIX	150
ACKNOWLEDGEMENTS	166
RECOMMENDED READING AND RESOURCES	168
BIBLIOGRAPHY	170
ABOUT THE AUTHOR	172

Jody Pignolet

To Wayne, Carli, Elaina and Glenn,
for continually inspiring my highest version of myself.

Jody Pignolet

Our greatest untapped natural resource might just be the indomitable human spirit buried beneath the eons of doubt, pain, fear and oppression. Like diamonds sitting quietly in the mines, our spirits patiently wait for that first crack of light to penetrate the darkness, for the journey that will lead us to our true and brilliant selves.

Jody Pignolet

THE IDEA

The idea is that what you have inside of you is what the world needs more of. You have the transformer, the nuclear reactor, the raw power, the Tony Stark/Ironman heart thing, the Holy Grail, inside of you. We all do. Each one of us has a 50-carat diamond waiting to be unearthed and the world needs it, YOU need it. It is you, your Authentic Self. Your pure essence is everything. It's what you've been looking for, it's what we've been looking for. This is the truth and I want you to know it; I want you to experience it and I want the world to have it.

Jody Pignolet

The privilege of a lifetime is to become who you truly are.

- Carl Jung

INTRODUCTION

I hold these ideas as truths:

1. I am amazing and so are you. We are, each and every one of us, without exception, divine, unique, fun, incredible, talented, loving and fabulous. That, in my belief system, is non-negotiable. And that truth of who you are, at your core, in your essence, is what I will from now on refer to as your Authentic Self.

2. Life told you a very different story about who you are and that's why you're not feeling/experiencing/expressing that awesomeness, or at least maybe not as often as you would like.

3. It is possible to connect more deeply with, and live more fully from, that Authentic Self.

4. It is possible to find and release the limiting ideas you have been given about who you are, leaving room for more and more of your Authentic Self to be lived and expressed.

5. Your authentic expression is your super-power. Living your true essence leads to you bringing your gifts, talents, and joy to the planet. It is, I believe, your most important contribution to your own happiness and to the world itself.

When I was 23 years old and at a 12-step meeting (finding ways to deal with my father's drinking habit), I had a Eureka moment. I still remember it as though it was yesterday; I was speaking with some new friends after the meeting and in that moment I clearly saw and felt how I was, and had been, modifying, adapting and contorting myself for each person I met so that I could be exactly who I imagined they would like. "Would you like me to be quieter, bubblier, or more serious, perhaps?" And in that moment of clarity I made a declaration; I said (yelled it, actually, to myself), "I just want to find out who I am and be that person with everyone!" Easier said than done, I have since learned, but nonetheless I have been on that sacred path of self-discovery and authenticity ever since.

Through my experiences in support groups, psychotherapy, spiritual and ecstatic awakenings, work with healers and my own independent study, I have spent the last 35+ years learning about my Authentic Self - what makes me tick, what brings me joy, and what I bring to the world. I have been able to explore finding and expressing my authentic voice through journaling, art, dance, screenwriting, singing, comedy, teaching, performing, relationship and parenting. Two of the highlights of my life are having the honor of helping to raise three very authentic humans and sharing a 38-year-long (so far) authentic and rewarding marriage. I am incredibly blessed and yes, luck and privilege have absolutely been factors, but my strong focus and intention have played just as big of a part in the richness of my life. My point here is that we all have the potential and possibility to live this much of life and so much more. I am definitely not done yet.

I am not special, I don't have anything that others don't have, I just happen to be living my Authentic Self and expressing it more and more because I am consciously uncovering it more and more. Like Michelangelo's approach to his David, I have been simply and consistently chipping away at the parts that are not authentically me.

I have learned through my process of self-discovery and through my path of spirituality that we are ALL amazing, magnificent beings at our essence and that it's only through life's wounds and the messages we have received that the magnificence gets buried and we live a much smaller, less vibrant version of who we truly are. Every single person is unique and has the potential to bring an amazing range of talents, gifts and qualities to the world, there is no exception, only the question of awareness, willingness, and the degree to which the Authentic Self has been buried.

We all want to connect with our essence, whether or not we are conscious of it, (it is our divine and earthly work, no matter where we are on the continuum of enlightenment) and when we do this it brings us joy and peace, AND, equally important, it brings something special, welcome and needed to the world; our awesomeness expressed.

Our job in this lifetime is not to shape ourselves into some ideal we imagine we ought to be, but to find out who we are already and become it.

- Steven Pressfield

AU-THEN-TIC-I-TY:

the quality of being real or true:

Based on the expectations of the world around me, I learned to keep certain aspects of myself hidden while I was growing up. I learned not to challenge authority (as I was the youngest of seven children, that basically meant everybody). I learned that I was too skinny, too sensitive, and that I cried too easily. I learned that girls don't play with trucks and that God was watching, taking notes and keeping score. These are a few examples of how my world has shaped me and discouraged my authentic expression. I held my tongue; I tried to hide my frequent tears out of shame; I went along with what others wanted as best as I could and, as a result, I had a nervous stomach, hunched shoulders, and propensity to make myself invisible.

My life force largely went into trying to feel okay in my stressful circumstances. Don't get me wrong, there were also many very lovely things about my childhood but trying to find the behaviors that would keep me from getting negative attention was my primary concern. These ideas and behaviors came with me into adulthood and influenced my choices. At 22 I married a man who was happy to lead and have me follow. And follow I did. I did just what was expected of women my age at the time, until I learned that there could be more and that I indeed wanted more. That is when I found that moment of clarity, of wanting to know who I was and what I wanted for my life.

Authenticity is a lifelong pursuit and an in-the-moment one. Authenticity, by its very nature, is different for everyone and can mean different things to different people. It can look like speaking your truth in a moment of conflict or vulnerability. It can mean wearing clothes that go against the current cultural trends. It can mean not going along with the crowd because that doesn't feel right. It can mean quitting law school to become an artist or quitting your tattoo gig to go to medical school. It can mean pursuing dance, music or science even if they are aren't as supported by the cultural binary gender expectations. It can mean being different and standing out or not standing out at all. It can mean making huge life changing decisions such as changing your physical appearance or form to align more with the gender you authentically feel you are, or it can be as small as feeling into what you're in the mood to eat. There is no one-size-fits-all and there are no rules or expectations attached to a path of authenticity. We don't do this for anyone else; it is neither a requirement nor a performance. We do this for ourselves, though others absolutely benefit, whether that ends up being an audience of one or one million.

When we talk about this idea of being "authentic" it can come across as an absolute, that you are meant to be 100% authentic, 100% of the time. It isn't about striving for perfection of some ideal of authenticity, but rather it's about acknowledging, being with and ultimately accepting what is real and true in you, in the moment. Absolute authenticity is not what I am pushing here but I would like to help you learn to be as authentic as you are able to be in any given moment. Even though I have been on this path for years, I still try to camouflage my tummy, I still sometimes conceal what I'm feeling and I'm still trying to straighten out those hunched shoulders that I'm embarrassed about. I go easy on myself while I continue trying to figure out what keeps me from my full acceptance and authenticity.

I'd also like to encourage you to forgive yourself for not being able to be authentic. There are many, many reasons for why this is so, the roots of which are not your fault. Being authentic today starts with you, letting yourself see what's true, what's going on and then having the choice of whether or not to share that with others. Having this awareness means that you get to make conscious, empowered choices about when, where and with whom you will share which parts of yourself until, and if, you are ready to fully embody and express that self all of the time.

Living an authentic life doesn't mean you magically get to have everything just the way you want it, but it will give you many more opportunities to dial your life into something that feels more like you. Living an authentic life also means you get to look for places in your life where you can experience the safety of being yourself and you get to notice and celebrate it when it happens, no matter how small. Pretty soon there will be many more of those moments.

The bottom line is that no other person gets to tell you who you are or what your life should look like. No one else gets to be the authority over what is inside and of what you are capable. That position is reserved for you and you alone. You get to enlist support from others but at the end of the day, you are the one who has the final say because the truth of who you are lives within you.

For a seed to achieve its greatest expression, it must come completely undone. The shell cracks, its insides come out and everything changes. To someone who doesn't understand growth, it would look like complete destruction.

- Cythnia Occelli

WHAT I WANT YOU TO KNOW

Why Now?

I feel like we are in a place and at a time in the world where there is a lot of focus on the frightening potential scenarios on the global horizon. We (especially young people) are being bombarded, through social media, with dreadful problems and horrific possible outcomes. If we are not connected to who we are and why we are here it can lead us to an overwhelming and depressing place. So many people are truly feeling afraid and hopeless. I take comfort in the belief that we are capable of so much more than we have been led to believe and that together we have everything we need in order to solve the problems of the world. At the very least, we have what we need to live a much more joyful existence while we are here, and that can't help but benefit everyone. No matter what is going on around us, uplifting our own selves and our individual worlds is the most helpful, most healing, and most intelligent thing we can do for ourselves and for each other.

There is no "Right Way"

As we are all unique, we all have different stories and we will be drawn organically to different ways of approaching these concepts. I cannot presume to tell you how to do this path of authenticity or that you should do it in any particular way, but I can offer guidance from my experience and I can bring forth certain concepts that have changed my perception and therefore my life. This book is not so much about me and how much I have learned, as it is about helping you on your unique, wildly varied, sacred path of self-discovery. And yet, it is about me because this book is my authentic expression, and through it, I get to celebrate the person I have become, or rather, re-discovered.

Side note: There is no right way to read this book either, only your way. If you are overwhelmed by the questions, skip them until you are ready for them. Feel free to skip or bounce around, following your curiosity. Given the nature of this book, however, I will recommend a little tool right off the bat: pay attention to what you feel emotionally and to what you experience in your body as you read it. Notice if there are parts that you find annoying or that you resist. Do you find yourself rolling your eyes? Why might that be? Are there passages that make you tear up or make your heart happy? Getting curious about your reactions to this material in particular, is a worthwhile pursuit, (and it will give you a great head start).

Notice too if you find yourself saying, "Yeah, but" at times, followed by the reasons why these ideas can't apply to you. This, again, is a result of past programming on what is or is not possible for you and getting curious about that can tell you a lot.

Please do not get too discouraged as you notice or see more about what you don't want in your life. The idea is not to focus on what isn't working but rather on what is needed for things to be as you would like them to be.

Most importantly, please notice if anything that I say in this book contributes to you feeling worse about yourself. If that is happening, simply get curious. What is going on in your being? What kinds of ideas are you telling yourself? I promise you that you are not *less-than* because you are not living your life differently right now.

This Is Not a "Fix you" Book

All that I offer is not about *fixing* you or making you more *acceptable*. There is nothing *wrong* with you. You are who you are, and you came to this current version of yourself honestly. Everything that you are today is beautiful and sacred, and it deserves to be honored as such. The point of this book is to get more of the *real* you for yourself and for the world. All that you have experienced has made you who you are today, and we don't want to dismiss any of that, but all that has gone into you becoming who you are today hasn't necessarily supported your authentic expression.

This Is Not an "Anti-caretaker" Book

I have no idea which characters in your life story contributed to your need to hide your Authentic Self, nor do I know in which ways they harmed you, but I want to be clear that they are not the focus of this book - you are. If you haven't already, you will likely have to deal with the fact that others in your life have had a negative impact on you. I want you to do that work, I want you to process that trauma and move through it so you can be free from it. I do not deny that people have harmed you, but I also am not intending to place blame or focus on these people through this book, simply because I want to keep my attention focused on you and what lives inside of you, on what in you wants to be seen and heard. It is not my place to put people on the hook nor let them off of it but, sadly, I can't imagine that there is a grown person walking on this earth today who hasn't on some level been taught that they are not okay just as they are, and who hasn't passed that learning onto others in some way.

This Is Absolutely a "Pro-you" Book

I don't know you, but I already know that there is very cool stuff inside. I don't know your story or what you have been through, but I know enough to honor you for continuing to show up in the world, at whatever level that may be. I am already on your side. I want to fluff you up, to celebrate you and, most importantly, I want to help you be able to celebrate yourself. I want to help you see what I would see if I were standing in front of you. I want you to know that the way you laugh or the way you don't want to express your needs or the way your hairline is receding are all lovable.

I want to inspire you to find out what else is in there. I want to encourage more exploration and I want to inspire more freedom. It's an amazing world out there, full of infinite possibilities for finding your unique signature, from hair color, piercings, and tattoos, to any kind of gender-fluid clothing imaginable. What else do you want to be? What could that look like? I want to see that. Mostly and most importantly, though, I simply want to help you claim your awesomeness and help you to be able to one day proclaim, as my youngest child likes to say, "I'm a goddamn delight!".

Remember that the minute you take your first step into the life of your dreams, the first to greet you there will be fear. Nod. Keep walking.
- Brianna Wiest

WHAT ELSE?

Fear and Resistance

Our beings come equipped with fear hard-wired into them. It is an integral part of our makeup for the most basic reason: survival. We have descended from beings for whom knowing the rules of behavior was a matter of life and death, a matter of being eaten by the tiger or not. As a young child you needed the acceptance of your caregivers for your very survival, and you needed to know which behaviors would ensure that. There are a million ways you've learned to keep yourself safe over the years. Staying safe very often also meant not acting in alignment with your Authentic Self, it meant keeping certain parts of yourself quiet or tucked away. It stands to reason that the more you explore ways to free up that Authentic Self today, the more that old fear will show its face and sound an alarm. It makes total sense and it is an intrusion.

There are many ways in which your being will likely resist this intention to connect more deeply with your Authentic Self, ways in which it will rebel, throw up roadblocks, distractions and self-sabotage. Your being might try to convince you that the work you are attempting to do will put your very life in jeopardy. This experience of fear and resistance is normal. It can look like: closing this book right now and then forgetting that you own it; dipping back into unhealthy patterns or relationships; falling into depression; falling ill; deciding you need to start a new and completely different project. It might take the form of negative and limiting self-talk such as: You're a fraud; That's impossible; Nobody wants what you have to say; Don't be so selfish; Don't be conceited; You're nothing special; and an old family favorite, Don't toot your own horn. Please, please, please be gentle with yourself, these governors have been put in place in order to help you feel safe. Safety needs to be created in a new way, both within yourself and in relationship with others. The process of daring to attempt to uncover these aspects of yourself must be treated with respect, gentleness and as much acceptance as you can muster. With that awareness you can recognize, bring to light, work with and release the ideas and fears you no longer need, the ones that do not serve you or the world. With that awareness you get to set free your unique and awesome true nature.

We all want to be seen and heard, we all need to be seen and heard and yet many of us fear being truly seen and heard. Being seen and heard in the past may have led to criticism and/or abuse. You might have the idea that being your Authentic Self will lead to more of this or that it will cost you love, relationships, success, status, or security. We can only imagine loss because this is what we were very likely taught and experienced. People in your life may subtly or not so subtly resist your authentic expression. What's more annoying to someone who has been stifled than someone who is free to express themselves? The recognition and understanding of that dynamic can foster empathy for both of you and it can help you to not take on the judgments and resistance of others.

You might encounter one or many dark nights of the soul; don't let that scare you away. This path of authenticity will call upon your courage. Inspiration and passion can fuel that courage when you recognize that you are indeed on your own quest for the holy grail. When you have become aware of and experienced for yourself the joy of your authenticity you will find that you are willing to endure that fear and discomfort, knowing it is in service of your true essence.

Every time I am going through a big growth spurt in my authenticity, I imagine that my marriage will blow up or something bad will happen to one of my children, because of it. I terrorize myself with these ideas, even after years of knowing better and after much experience to the contrary, that's how powerful the fear and resistance can be. And yet, I have persisted because it is the thing I want most.

Your Evolution

Personal evolution isn't linear, nor is it logical. My own path has been neither linear nor logical. I am not offering you a "10 easy steps to transformation" kind of a path where you can predict exactly what will come next. It can be helpful to know that there will be times when it doesn't make sense what you are being urged to address or to what you are finding yourself drawn. The powers that be (or whatever you look to beyond yourself, if anything), and your own higher self, have a bigger picture and a higher wisdom for how to help you evolve. We don't know what in you is ready to come up, be exposed or be expressed, nor when.

Many of the limiting beliefs you uncover about yourself will fall away quickly while others will have layers that will get shed bit by bit over years and years. The path of authenticity is a long game. We have built this version of ourselves over time and it might take time to tear down the barriers we have put in place, these walls to our true selves. Big shifts can and do happen quickly and then life can sometimes feel a lot like the movie "Groundhog Day", revisiting the same idea over and over again. Though it may feel like the same old place, you are becoming a different person every day and, as the indigenous people say, "You can't step in the same river twice". In other words, you can't help but evolve. It is a process; start small and keep it simple, if you can. Your progress and experience can lead to trust and faith in yourself and in the wisdom and brilliance of the process.

Creating Safety

We can get very impatient once we are on the scent or the trail of becoming a *better version* of ourselves, wanting change to happen now. As I said before, there is nothing *wrong* with you that needs to be fixed, nothing that must be changed to make you a more acceptable person, a person more worthy of love. That is not the point of this book or this path. You might be yearning for changes because you don't like yourself or parts of yourself, believing that there *is* something wrong with you, that there is another version of yourself that is more lovable. That is simply the result of taking on some of the falsehoods you were told about who you are. You came to be the person you are today honestly and organically, but you simply may not be feeling in alignment with your true self. It is crucial to understand the difference between trying to change based on an outside view of what is right or acceptable versus helping who you truly are to come to the surface. The former will never really scratch the itch, the latter will feel like water in the desert.

Being able to familiarize ourselves with the concept of unconditional self-acceptance is a key foundation for this path. We each have our own particular preferences, traits, quirks, idiosyncrasies. Some are due to trying to contort ourselves to fit in but some are just genuinely because of who we are, because of our authentic essence. Regardless of how or where these traits originate, we deserve acceptance from others and most especially, most importantly, from ourselves.

A few groups in particular that have been societally encouraged to hide (aside from, of course, those who don't have the majority skin color) are those with gender identities or sexual orientations outside of the perceived societal "norm"; those with spiritual, psychic, or paranormal gifts or experiences outside of the mainstream experience; and those who live with addiction and/or mental health issues. Society, in general, has been lacking in acceptance of these differences, though basically any trait or characteristic that is on either side of "average" or "normal", and which subjects one to judgment, ridicule, and marginalization, can feel like a curse and something to be hidden. We humans have made some headway concerning tolerance, but we still have a very long way to go. (I notice many of the younger generations have this understanding organically and are showing the rest of us how to do it.) If you fall into any category, on any level, that is outside of the cultural/societal norms, averages, and preferences, I see you and I encourage you to bring fierce love and acceptance or find it outside of yourself for now. You deserve to be yourself; the world will be a much better place for it. We all lose when you hide your Authentic Self away.

What are You Really up For?

In the early 1940s a psychologist named Abraham Maslow shared with the world his idea of the hierarchy of human needs. At the very basic level of his model are the physiological needs: food, water, and shelter. He built upon that, believing that unless the basic human needs were met a person couldn't access the more enriching experiences of life, such as connection with others. At the top of this hierarchy he placed the need for self-actualization – for reaching one's potential. If we are to be all that we can be, our beings must be able to feel at ease, and our basic needs must be satisfied. If we have been raised in a traumatic/stressful environment, if we are currently living in such an environment, our nervous system is very likely spending most of its time on high alert, leaving us unavailable for more subtle awareness, for connection, or for creative pursuits. If indeed your nervous system is fried, as is true for so many of us, you need gentleness, nurturing and kindness. Recognizing the impact of past and present trauma/stress on our beings and finding ways to counteract that reality is vital to our pursuit of authenticity.

There is a lot being written today about trauma, its impact on the nervous system and how to bring the nervous system back on-line. The more time we can spend in a state of ease and nervous system regulation, the more access we have to our intuition, intellect, creativity, and generosity, and most importantly, the more we are able to be aware of when we are in alignment with our Authentic Selves and the more we are able to make different choices when we find that we are not in alignment. When our nervous system is regulated, we also have an increased capacity to handle whatever comes up along the way, when life gets challenging.

Lack of safety is the very thing that has prevented us from expressing our authenticity for all of these years, so it is imperative that we afford ourselves the safety now that we needed back then. It starts with an intention to have our own backs and to practice kindness and acceptance toward ourselves. We don't need any more harshness, no one does. It starts with tending to our own fears and stress. It starts with letting these parts, which have been in hiding, know that they will be loved and accepted by you, before you are ready to bring them to the world. Having people in your world who also intend to love and accept you as you are is a priceless gift. Sometimes they are the people who can show us how it is done as they see and accept our Authentic Selves, way before we do.

We Don't Do This Alone

These ideas are ideas of the soul - our deeper, eternal and divine selves - not the mind or body (though they do play a part) and I believe that these souls are a part of something bigger than our individual selves. Though that is what I believe, it is not a requirement that you believe in spirituality, a higher self or higher power, or that your particular spiritual beliefs align with mine for the concepts in this book to apply to or be embraced by you. You are sincerely invited to discard anything that doesn't feel like truth to you.

I grew up with a very structured and religious explanation of who we humans are and what we are doing here on Earth. I learned that we are here to *be good* and do good so that when we are ready to meet our maker we will be well received, so we will end up in the *good* place. I was taught the notion of *original sin*, that we are here trying to redeem the fact that we are born flawed, sinful humans and that we must work hard to overcome these dark human natures of ours. I was also taught that we should put others first and ourselves last. These notions were intended to help me, but I have found them inherently limiting. During my experiences in 12-step programs I was introduced to the concept of "a god of our understanding". There I was encouraged to expand my perception and my imagination, of what a higher power could be, what that could feel like, and to find a vision that felt true and authentic to me. My personal experiences with the god of my understanding have expanded my faith, my heart and my compassion for myself and others. I see all of these ideas as spiritual ones and more expansive than those of any specific religion. As singer Michael Franti says, "God is too big for just one religion."

The unseen world is bigger, more loving and more complex than I will likely ever understand though it is not so important to me today to know exactly what form God, the universe or the unseen world takes. There is a benevolent force of light and love behind the scenes, call it what you want, and we are created from those same essential ingredients. Whether we are aware of them or not, we also have unseen beings who provide us with support in becoming the highest versions of ourselves. I love to refer to these unseen beings on my team as my Spiritual Support Squad, and they include ancestors and loved ones, guides, angels and saints. You might call them grandmothers, grandfathers, guardian angels, spirit guides. Other cultures have different names, but just about every culture acknowledges and represents the unseen world in some way.

My belief system holds that each of us existed before this present incarnation and that we came into this one with lessons to learn; aspects of our consciousness to develop and evolve; experiences to have; and other beings to encounter. We work together (consciously and unconsciously) with our unseen helper beings to accomplish all of that.

We can't possibly fathom how loved we are and how much support there is for our evolution. It has been my experience many times, that these unseen beings have been helping me to reconnect with my essence of love and light and that when I intend to partner with them miracles, synchronicities, and magic are possible and do occur. That can look like me being nudged (or sometimes pushed) in a certain direction; being guided to the left when I thought I was going right. It can look like certain people magically turning up in my life just when I need them. The more open one is to the idea that your helpers are actually working for your highest good, and for your evolution and intention, the more you can begin to consciously join forces and become even more productive and powerful.

As I said, it is not at all necessary that you view the world or your existence in the same way, though I find a belief in something larger than oneself to be very valuable, ultimately, you are the authority of your connection with yourself and whatever forces you view as beyond yourself. I am simply presenting a perspective, a view or possibility for you to consider and a context for how authenticity fits into how I see who we are and what we're doing here on this planet. Which brings me back to the focus of this book; we are, each of us, created of pure love, for pure love. It is what exists within each of us regardless of how many layers obscure it. I believe that it is our soul's desire to live from these truths and manifest our highest expression of pure love and light.

Consciously Choosing This

I have seen a lot of evidence that this process of becoming oneself can happen and does happen, organically beyond our conscious awareness, in many ways and at many times. Unseen forces shift things, helping us to adapt and change. But once we have stepped consciously onto this path, once we have truly claimed our intention of living our Authentic Selves "no matter what", everything changes. Then we can start truly co-creating, seeing the magic and working with the abundance of support that exists for each one of us.

I have felt the need to re-up my commitment to this path many times. I have written my intention simply in my journal, I have created vision boards, I have created ceremony, and I have declared it to my friends and to my family. I have said my prayers on the laundry room floor, in the shower and on the mountain top; there is no right or wrong way to claim your intention or speak it to yourself and the universe. The only thing that matters is your pure desire.

Traveling a path of authenticity may mean that unpleasant changes occur, but once we have chosen this path deliberately, everything then becomes an opportunity for growth, everything becomes an opportunity to discover what is and isn't you. I like to say that when a part of me is champing at the bit to move forward, there is another part of me holding onto the back of my pants with her heels dug in. There have been many times when I feared that the changes which I wanted to make in myself would turn my world upside down. I needed to find the courage and make the scary choice to move forward anyway.

I generally think it is much more painful to stay stagnant and struggling than it is to grow. If I am going to be uncomfortable then I would prefer that my discomfort help move me along my path as opposed to helping me stay content in my small, safe world. There have been many invitations to run from this path out of fear. For sure there have been times when I wished that I could go back to sleep or just coast, but every time I claimed this as my path, as my intention, my being (and my spiritual support squad) cheered me on and delivered more clarity, more synchronicity, and more magic, and I was able to move a little further on down the road, toward my full Authentic Self.

There are beautiful wild forces within us.
Let them turn millstones inside
Filling bushels that reach to the sky.
- St. Francis of Assisi

SECTION I: Your Amazing Self

You are divine. This is what lives inside of you, it is your animating force within your earthly body. You are made up of the very stuff of the gods with your own unique energetic signature and it is pure bliss to live this truth. It is likely that you aren't living this truth, (at least not as often as you would like), because of all of the untruths you have been taught growing up, truths that now obscure your amazingness and distort your perception of who you are, (in some cases to something that barely resembles human in your eyes). These untruths and misinformation have been disseminated by very credible (to you at the time) sources such as your caregivers and teachers, your community, your religious influences, TV, movies, social media, and society in general. You have also manufactured a lot of it in your own mind because you have been trying, with your limited understanding at the time, to make sense of things in your world. Nonetheless, your pure essence is holy, radiant, creative and wise. Feel that. It is in there, in you, and in every other human on the planet.

Providing this wasn't trained out of you, you can find joy and wonder just looking at a newborn baby. They are straight out of the heavenly realm and it shows. Imagine that tiny being coming into the world. Imagine its parents celebrating its arrival, expressing their joy that this little being has found its way into their lives. Everything about the faces, voices and demeanors of the parents says, "We are so happy that you are here". When the eyes of the child meet the eyes of the parents, they see pure love and joy reflected back at them. This baby knows/feels from its first day in the world that it is loved for no other reason than that it exists.

This is unconditional love and acceptance and it is what we might imagine as an ideal scenario in an ideal world. Sometimes, many times, a child's entrance into the world doesn't look anything like that. And even if it does look like that at the beginning, that expression of unconditional love can wane. When the baby won't sleep or can't stop crying or when she grows a little older and has opinions of her own, or when he wants his nails painted too, the messages from the outside start to change. And when that happens a series of judgments, labels, and ideas make their way into the child's being, as truth. You're a pain in the neck; you stress mommy out; you're too loud; grandma doesn't love you when you're angry; good girls don't do that. That little person has begun to believe a story about themselves that simply isn't true. That little person can begin to feel shame about aspects of themselves and begin to hide them from the world and from themselves or they can try to shape themselves into something they believe is more acceptable, more lovable. There are endless examples: Children stuffing their anger because it isn't safe to express it; middle schoolers desperately trying to fit in with the cool kids; teens famously living lives completely different from the ones their parents believe they are living. In high school, I tried to hide my chronic sadness behind a smiling, laughing façade.

In addition to these messages of non-acceptance, the traumatic and dramatic events that take place during a child's life can dramatically alter the way that child sees themselves and the world. Caretakers leave or die; someone is abusive; siblings are born, or existing siblings have special needs, to name just a few. The safe bubble that may have existed for a child is destroyed in the course of a life, potentially leaving that being with altered and very limited ideas about themselves and the world. None of this happens through the fault of a child but it is the child who bears the weight of these unfortunate occurrences.

Pure Essence

Despite all of those potential pitfalls, kids can also be great teachers by showing us how to be authentic. Have you ever had a child spontaneously perform something for you? Have you ever been to a child's music or dance recital? Do you care if the kid messes up? Probably not, because you are witnessing that kid's authentic expression. Again, unless this was trained out of you, unless you were shamed for your organically imperfect authentic expression, for singing off pitch, for being *too much*, for marching to the beat of your own drum.

My kids went to a Waldorf School where every year a talent show was held. My youngest kid, at nine years old, decided to sing "Tomorrow" from the musical Annie. They (this person is non-binary and their pronouns are they/them) were so inspired by this idea that they figured out how to download a karaoke version from the computer and burn it onto a CD (this was 2007); they got themselves signed up for the audition; they received "notes" from the directors and when the day of the show came, they delivered a sincere, heart-felt performance, and the audience loved it. I watched in awe (and some envy). I was already on board with this theme of authenticity so fortunately I didn't try to talk them out of it, but I was tempted to out of my fear that they would embarrass themselves (and by association, me). Instead I was inspired to be braver and more authentic myself.

A few years later at the talent show, there was a 10-year-old boy who sang a killer rendition of Johnny Cash's "Burning Ring of Fire". Can you imagine? The audience erupted when he finished. We grown-ups thought these kids were so brave and so extraordinary, but they were just doing what they did, expressing their authentic awesomeness. They were doing what we all can do, in some way, but may have been told that we couldn't.

Believing that we couldn't or can't do these things does not negate the fact that your talents, dreams, gifts, and authentic expressions still live inside of you. So much still lives inside of you and despite how it may feel, these aspects never die. Despite how much time has passed, it is never too late to bring them back to the surface, bringing much more joy into your life.

Side note: It can be too easy to imagine that this can't be true of you because of your age. I want to stress that age has very little to do with true authenticity as your true essence does not grow old. I am practically the poster child for "it's never too late". Most of the joyful authentic experiences I have had have happened after turning forty and as I said earlier, I am definitely not done yet. My late Aunt Lillian has been my role model as she revamped her life at 92!

Unfortunately, without all of this perspective, most of us end up living a much smaller life and being a more ordinary version of ourselves. Remember, that is not something anyone needs to feel shame or less-than about. Who you are today is worthy of love and acceptance no matter what you and your life look like or which version of yourself you are currently living.

The Iceberg

The metaphor of an iceberg is overused to be sure, but it is apt here when we consider the depth and breadth of who you truly are. There is so much more to you than meets the eye. So much more hidden beneath the surface. I love this thought and it's one of the ideas I love to explore with others. Who is in there? What treasures are buried in the depths of your being? What stories do you have? I am in a writer's group where every other woman is older than I am, and I am regularly delighted by the colorful stories of their past experiences and what they are up to in the present; stories you couldn't possibly know or guess just by looking at them. I love learning about the struggles they have had and the dreams they have fulfilled. I believe that every person has many stories and that all of those stories are worthy of being heard.

    I practice a mindfulness modality called Authentic Relating and one of the activities I learned to do with others is called "If You Really Knew Me". The idea is to give others the opportunity to choose what they want the listener to know about them. It can be as simple as "If you really knew me, you would know that I can't start my day without coffee." or something deep and personal such as, "If you really knew me you would know that I have been to hell and back." Getting to witness people while they sit with themselves and choose what it is they really want me to know about them in that moment - getting to watch them muster the courage to share, no matter how deep or how shallow - is an exquisite experience. To watch others while they witness this is equally beautiful. This is the kind of stuff I live for, it's my rocket fuel. It is a privilege and an honor to be shown what most people keep below the surface but can feel safe enough to share in these moments. It can be scary and edgy for all involved but I never fail to feel joy and reverence when someone shares with me who they really are. The awe and amazement I feel when someone shows me what lives inside is what I imagine a doctor might feel when they see the literal insides of a person for the first time.

You think you know what is in there, in you or someone else, but very often you can get surprised by what lies beneath the surface. That's the fun of all of this. My oldest daughter is a great example of this. She was always a cautious, timid, child. She hated leaving the house to go to school but somewhere along the line she began to see that not only did she want to leave the house, but she also wanted to leave the country. She is now a very brave and adventurous international teacher. She didn't hold onto that story of being cautious and timid, instead she heard a deeper story of an adventurer within and went with that one.

I knew a man who was already a very skilled professional piano player and composer but one day, while drawing with markers alongside his two young daughters he discovered a latent talent as a visual artist. Practically overnight he began drawing beautiful, intricate and colorful landscapes. He didn't know that was in there, but he definitely said, "Yes!" to it when it surfaced. Those who get to see his art are gifted too.

I love thinking about the potential not yet accessed. I love learning about child prodigies and people with savant syndrome because I believe it shows us our true human potential and what is possible if we could get a lot of the false programming out of the way. I believe it isn't just reserved for a few exceptional beings. We all have our own brand of brilliance and we are all connected to and are allowed access to the incredible, abundant universal mind.

The Cost of Self Denial

It takes a tremendous amount of energy to suppress your Authentic Self, to keep it below the surface, and that effort takes its toll on the body, the spirit, relationships and life direction. That kind of denial of oneself can lead to depression, illness, divorce, addiction, lethargy, and even jail. When our beings work this hard to suppress who we are, that suppressed energy can instead come out sideways and in inappropriate ways, ranging from anger or deception, to violence toward ourselves or others. When our beings need to devote energy and attention to repressing aspects of ourselves, we have less energy available for creativity, fun, collaboration, generosity, and connection. The good news is that those are the things waiting for you as you live more and more of your Authentic Self. When I decided that I was going to find out who I was and be that person no matter what, I did not know that that would include more than just how I showed up with and for myself or in my relationships, but also how I got to track, unearth, and express my own unique gifts and talents, bringing me more joy than I imagined. I didn't know that the dreams I had as a little kid would actually and finally get to manifest. I have worked through a lot of my fear and resistance and have had the exhilarating experiences of singing, dancing and doing comedy on stage. I started a YouTube channel. I'm writing a book, for heaven's sake! None of that would have, or could have, happened if I hadn't searched for, trusted in, and said *yes* to what was inside of me.

There is something real in you. There is something beautiful in you. If you want to be mesmerized by beauty, be mesmerized by the beauty that is within you. If you want to understand something, understand yourself.

If you want to love, love this beautiful breath that comes into you. If you do this, you will be given a gift of peace, joy, love – not in thoughts, not in words, but in feeling. And that is no ordinary gift.

- Prem Rawat

SECTION II - Part 1: Getting to the Real You

You are unique and amazing. Is this starting to sound redundant? I know that I have mentioned that once or twice already but when you consider how many times you might have heard the opposite; I think I can't say it too many times. There is only one of you. Sit with that just for a minute. There is only one of you and I believe that you were made unique on purpose, for a whole host of beautiful reasons.

You can tell you aren't like anyone else just by looking in the mirror (unless you're an identical twin) but it can be hard to imagine that your uniqueness is actually a gift. You might have been told that you were weird, you might have been told that you should have a straighter nose, or a quieter voice, but you don't, this is who you are. And it goes way beyond the physical, external characteristics. What experiences have you had? What do you like to do or learn about? Do you notice that you aren't interested in the same things as everyone else? There really is no *everyone else*; every single person on the planet is different and while you might share some interests with others, no one else has the unique combination of traits, physical characteristics and experiences that you have. I used to think that was a bad thing. I used to think that I was less-than because I wasn't like those who appeared to be cooler, smarter, funnier or more athletic than I was. I genuinely didn't know that anything about me was interesting or worth noting. That is how conditioned I was to think that being just like others was the objective, and that going along with societal expectations was the way to be happy.

Authenticity Applied – I Love the Wind

I remember being around eight or nine years old and playing outside on our front lawn when a cold front blew in with a lot of wind. I remember my being coming to life with all of that wind and I remember my fervent desire to move with it. I felt so happy and alive and connected to nature as I ran around the yard, being moved by the gusts. I ran inside to tell my mother about how much fun I was having playing in the wind. Because she was overwhelmed with her duties of raising seven children, she wasn't able to witness my joy. She just didn't get it and in fact, I think she was a little snarky, so I told myself it didn't mean anything, and I probably went into the den to watch TV. I now know that I do love the wind, and nature, dogs, horses, moving my body, and so many other things. I had some awareness of that when I was younger, but it wasn't until I was an adult that I understood what it meant to claim that awareness as something important, something valid, for my individual self. I eventually began to grasp that recognizing that these things made me happy meant that I could and would consciously bring them into my life more, therefore inviting more aliveness and more happiness.

Res-o-nance: the condition in which an object or system is subjected to an oscillating force having a frequency close to its own natural frequency.

Everyone and everything has a vibrational frequency and people, places, things and ideas vibrating at a similar frequency are said to be in resonance. When we are in resonance with a person, place, thing, or idea it feels harmonious to us. The opposite is also true, leading to a feeling of dissonance. The feeling of this resonance is evidence that we are in harmony or in alignment with a person, place, thing or idea and that it exists much more peacefully within our beings. When we are in alignment, our beings - physically, mentally, emotionally and spiritually, feel well. When we are not in resonance or alignment our beings feel much more dissonance, more stress, tension and dis-ease. For instance, me writing these words brings me joy, it's what I love and want to do. What don't I want to do? Work with numbers in an office all day or drive a bus. (Thankfully, some people do.)

Believing in the idea that people, places, things, ideas and experiences have the power to make us feel alive and joyful when they are in harmony with our true essence can dramatically change the trajectory of one's life. Bringing this to your awareness means that you have more control over your happiness and your life direction.

It is possible, and it is worthwhile to learn more about what those sources of resonance are for yourself: what do you love; when are you having the most fun; what brings you joy and peace; what lights you up; what do you love doing and what do you have to offer the world? It is the most self-loving thing you can do to find new and different sources of reflection, different from those old ideas you took on, about who you are, what's possible, and what you have to give.

Side note: It is important to mention that I am referring to experiences that are not fueled by chemicals. Being in a chemically altered state can bring on feelings of euphoria, peace, or lightness but it is important to acknowledge that those states are temporary and can also come with a cost. Recognizing that you organically come equipped with uplifting feelings and that they are your birthright; having faith that it is possible to experience them (or remembering hopefully that you have experienced them) in a sober state, can be a revelation for some. Fortunately, there is a class of chemicals that research has shown can have a lasting positive impact. Clinical use of psychedelics has been shown to help people open up to a more positive, more expansive mindset and can expose people to a broader perspective, one that is helpful when trauma or disappointment has closed off thoughts of a brighter possibility. Exciting new treatments are currently in the works and I am looking forward to the resulting expansion and healing and the impact of that on the world.

We all have had experiences of this resonance and we may even have noted it; we might be able to recall those instances when we organically felt alive, super-charged, blissed out, ecstatic, or profoundly peaceful. They're available everywhere and anytime; anything from standing by the ocean watching a sunset, to watching a wholesome and heart-opening commercial can elicit such an experience.

I love the idea of tuning in even more to what that feels like. I love tracking what is happening when you come to life, getting to understand what is happening out there and inside of you, so that you can learn to recognize it in the moment. By intending to bring this to conscious awareness you can begin to learn precisely what has this lovely impact on your being, allowing you to create and call in more and more such moments. With this focus you get to learn about who you are and what makes you come to life.

What does it feel like for you in these moments? Do you experience goose bumps, chills, electricity in your being, heart racing, expansiveness, awe, coming to life? Do you feel deep peace, or does it feel like coming home? Do you tear up or does what you're experiencing make your heart go pitter-patter?

If you are like me, you were taught not to trust these very feelings. You may have been taught to be suspicious or wary of feelings of excitement, of joy, of euphoria. You might have learned that disappointment comes after happiness so it's better to stay away from happiness to avoid feeling let down. Instead, I believe that these uplifting feelings are the very signals our beings can give us when we are on the right track, when we are experiencing resonance with our Authentic Selves. This is our being recognizing itself and saying, "Yes, that is me!" and the amazing thing is that our beings come factory-installed with our own barometer or gauge to help us recognize this resonance. Our beings know who we truly are, and they absolutely recognize this kind of alignment and resonance.

Where might you have noticed those feelings? In the expansiveness of nature; while traveling; having new experiences; moving your body; or perhaps with a new person? It can be experienced with something small and seemingly insignificant such as excitement over picking out something from a menu or something life changing in the case of recognizing a new and important person. A simple example I discovered years ago has to do with buying clothes. It might sound too shallow to be of value but stay with me. I noticed I could be in the dressing room at a store, trying on top after top. Yes, that one looks good, that one fits well, or I like the color of that one, but then I would put on something and my whole being would come to life. I would have an "Oh, yes!" experience. That is the reaction I am looking for and that is the only thing I should buy. I will sometimes try to talk myself into the other ones, but in my experience, the rest of them, the ones that "look good on paper", won't get worn if I do buy them but the one that truly makes my heart go pitter-patter will undoubtedly be a favorite and worth my money.

That feeling of my heart going pitter-patter, as I like to call it, is my being letting me know that we have resonance. I don't even have to understand it, it doesn't have to make sense to my rational mind, it is simply my job to notice it, acknowledge it and go along with it if I am able. Remember, people, places, things, ideas and experiences can all elicit this ding, ding, ding response on any scale. Our job is simply to track that response, that feeling, to notice when and where it comes up and to say, "Yes!" to it if we are able.

Resonance in your being might feel like:
Goosebumps
Deep peace
Coming home
Chills
Ecstasy
Breathlessness
Tummy tickles
Floating on air
Walking on air
Expansiveness

You might have other examples that I haven't thought of. When and where do you notice them and what do they feel like?

Recognizing Yourself

Aside from paying attention to your inner barometer in the moment (or by looking at past experiences for more understanding), you can consciously seek, connect with, and learn more about your Authentic Self. You have probably read something about your astrological "Sun sign" for example, it is one of the most mainstream ways in which people can get a little glimpse into their uniqueness through astrology. If your sun sign is in Virgo (if you were born in late August or the first two thirds of September) for instance, you likely enjoy order. For me, astrology has helped me better understand myself and others. It has also helped me fine-tune where to focus my energy and has shown me in which areas of my life I am likely to get stuck.

There are many more layers to astrology and what it can tell you about yourself, but this is just one possible tool, there are many other different modalities available in the world as well. I am familiar with and have had experiences with numerology, tarot, personality or psychological testing, aura colors, Enneagram, psychic readings, psychotherapy, just to name a few. The point is, we are unique individuals at our core, based on so many aspects of our existence, from when and where we were born; our ancestry; the experiences we have had, and ancient and modern tools exist specifically to help you learn more about what makes up your Authentic Self. We're not letting someone tell us who we are, rather we are exposing ourselves to possibilities of who we might be and giving our beings the opportunity to recognize that as the truth or not.

There are so many different modalities and practitioners available for connecting with your authenticity that it is possible for you to find which ones really speak to or resonate with you. Let yourself tune into which ones you feel curious about or are drawn to. If it resonates, you are more likely to trust, benefit from and enjoy whatever it is you are pursuing. My relationship with exercise helped me learn this concept.

After many abandoned exercise programs, I realized that I needed to find ways to move my body that I actually enjoyed otherwise I wouldn't stick with them. Actually, it was a revelation to realize that I could exercise my body and have fun and feel joy at the same time, so conditioned was I to the ideas of discipline, hard work and *no pain, no gain*. Believing that I could take care of my body and light myself up at the same time led me to swimming, dancing, taking long walks, and the practice of yoga, all of which give me energy, make me feel alive and joyful, and contribute to the overall health of more than just my body. That same idea can help you find which path, which tools and which practitioners are right for your exploration of yourself.

Awareness is Key

All of this self-exploration relies on your awareness of what you are actually experiencing. Mindfulness and embodiment practices offer ways to anchor you and your awareness, helping you to become more acquainted with yourself and what you're experiencing in any given moment. The practice of Yoga has had a profound impact on my connection to my Authentic Self through valuing and encouraging self-acceptance and by teaching me how to find comfort in the present moment, the only moment there is. Without a doubt, the biggest positive impacts have been the deepening of my connection to my physical body and the increase in my ability to be aware of what I am experiencing in each moment.

The practice of slowing down and mindfully tuning into what you are experiencing in the moment, any moment, is a foundational tool for authenticity and yet those words, "mindfulness" and "presence" have been used so often lately that they may have lost their potency. Or perhaps they trigger fear and resistance in you. So many of us have been trying to escape what we're experiencing, why would we want to bring our focus to it? Sitting quietly can understandably sound like torture to some. You can take comfort in knowing that there is more than one way to cultivate presence and awareness. You can find some of those alternative practices in the Appendix.

Awareness, however you get there, is the key to having the option of choosing a different way forward. Once again, I am not advocating an absolute; it's a practice, a little-by-little building of noticing skills, which will help you recognize, celebrate and choose what is happening in each moment.

Side note: Awareness, as I refer to it here, must be distinguished from hypervigilance. While we want to build the capacity to recognize what is happening in the present moment, that awareness is not born out of anxiety but rather out of an open and curious state. Hypervigilance, however, is an extreme level of anxious awareness adopted as a coping mechanism in order to constantly track and monitor potential threats.

Authenticity Applied – Giving Voice

Many years ago I had the wonderful opportunity of participating in a six week class based on "The Artist's Way" (a book and course on recovering one's creativity by Julia Cameron) and I was able to reclaim my inner artist by working through the old tightly-held judgments I had around my own talent as a visual artist. Most importantly though, I discovered, or rather, remembered, my love and affinity for writing via the practice of "Morning Pages". Cameron teaches the practice of writing three continuous and uncensored pages of stream of consciousness flow. This was one of the biggest contributors to my seeing who and what was inside of me. I was able to give a voice to myself, my thoughts, my fears and my creativity. I was able to safely give a voice (and acceptance) to all of that within myself long before I was able to share it with anyone else.

This level of exploration and inquiry into who you are is available on every level from what you like to eat for breakfast, to how you like to be in relationship with others, to what you have to contribute to the world. There are modalities and practitioners available out there to assist you with your quest. Your internal guidance system is calibrated to this intention and always has been.

Resources for Self-Discovery:

Astrology
Love languages
Aura reading
Numerology
Personality testing
Psychological testing
Psychotherapy
Enneagram
Journaling
Morning pages (see Appendix)
Creation writing (see Appendix)
Mediums
Psychics
Healers
Shamans
Body work
Sound Healing
Akashic Record Readings
Emotional Freedom Technique (aka Tapping)
Internal Family Systems Therapy
Family Constellation Therapy

Resurrecting Your Dreams

When you were young, you might have felt inspired to dream about your future. Perhaps you told someone about those dreams and were told in return that your dreams weren't possible and perhaps you may have shut it all down right then and there. If there was no dreaming because the environment was too stressful, I offer my condolences and my reassurance that it is not too late for what I am about to say next. My experience is that those true soul dreams don't actually die. It might not be exactly the way we imagined it with our five or ten-year-old minds, but something about the essence of that desire was true and is likely true about you and your desires today. Discovering and nurturing those dreams opens up yet another avenue for joy in your life.

Authenticity Applied – Our Younger Selves Know

For most of my childhood, I can remember loving singing, I sang everywhere and in fact, I had fantasies of being *discovered* and performing on stage. That might have seemed natural if I had been a loud or gregarious child, but I wasn't, I was painfully shy, sensitive and very anxious. At mealtimes I would hide under the table if anyone so much as looked at me sideways. I didn't tell anyone about my dream, that was too risky, and my parents didn't have the resources to support voice or acting lessons for me regardless. But that dream of mine did not die, it was like a zombie in the way it would not die, despite all of the impediments. In high school I auditioned for singing groups and musicals but didn't *make it*. I simply didn't know how to do any of it well. I took voice lessons on and off in my adulthood, but it wasn't until I was in my forties that I finally supported myself in making my performance dreams come true. I was able to first join our local amateur choir; whose safe environment gave me the courage to start studying voice seriously.

Years later, cut to me standing on stage, belting out a musical number, complete with backup dancers, in front of an audience of 500 people. The second I stepped on that stage I felt as though I belonged there and that everything was going to be all right. It was, and I had the time of my life. It was truly a peak experience for me, and I guess you could say that I finally discovered myself.

My middle child is another great example of trusting your childhood desires. When she was small the game she loved most to play, whenever she could rally her siblings or the neighborhood kids, was school. One of her favorite outings with me was going to the teacher supply store. She also loved art as a child and ended up majoring in art in college. That surprised me because I was so sure she was going to study education. After she graduated from college, she wasn't sure of which direction to head, but a teaching assistant job at a Montessori school *just happened* to land in her lap and she took it. The next year the art teacher left the school leaving the position available. Guess who applied and is now an amazing and inspired art teacher? If she had simply studied education, the track that "made sense" instead of art, the track her heart wanted, she might have completely missed that art teacher opportunity and experience.

The Gift of Envy

Paying attention to when you are feeling jealousy or envy is a fabulous way of helping you see which desires and dreams you might be harboring. I believe that these feelings tell you what you want in your life. Again, not necessarily exactly how it is happening for the other person but something about what they are experiencing resonates with you and your green eyes are trying to bring that to your awareness. You are jealous or envious because you want something. Many of us have been taught to feel shame about jealousy or envy, but I believe the root of those feelings is a legitimate and valid desire worthy of our attention.

Authenticity Applied – The Speedo

When I was a child, I was envious of my best friend and her purple Speedo swim team bathing suit. I couldn't imagine how she could possibly swim so far and for so long, I didn't believe I had that in me, but I still wanted that cool suit. Years later (many, many years later) I caught myself watching a swimmer gracefully do laps in the pool. I noticed that what I was feeling as I watched was envy. I already knew that I came alive when I was in water so it occurred to me that I might actually like to properly learn to swim. I signed myself up for adult swim lessons, faced some old shame and fears, and opened myself up to a whole new avenue for fitness, adventure and fun. I competed in masters swim meets and completed two 1.76-mile-long open water swims, all in my own very cool Speedo.

Some of the people whom I currently envy or have envied over the years:
People who are traveling
Singers when they are singing full out
Storytellers
Experts who can stand up in front of other people and talk easily about what they know
Filmmakers
Public speakers
Musicians
Anyone performing on stage
Published authors

Whom do you envy?

A Treasure Chest of Judgments

We are all living in a world full of judgments, from tiny to huge, overt and covert, and our judgments, when we are willing to acknowledge and own them, can tell us so much about what ideas we have been taught and to which ones we are holding fast. When we judge something outside of ourselves as wrong or bad there is a reason for that judgment. Objectively we can't really know what is wrong or bad as there are so many variables involved in any circumstance but if we dissect what goes on inside of ourselves, what is activated and what belief or idea underlies that, we can find tremendously valuable information. We can learn, for example, what we value, what we need or want, and/or what we fear.

Once those judgments are out in the open, we have the opportunity to claim them or let them go if they are not serving us. I was taught to judge attention seeking as bad and people who tried to get attention as, well, lame. The tricky thing with that was that I was in desperate need of attention. I needed to set that judgment aside so that I could be free to get the attention I needed. Once I could accept that we all need attention and that needing attention was completely valid, I was able to help myself fulfill that need and I was able to forgive others for seeking attention, as well.

Judgment in our culture is insidious. The arbitrary values we place on human beings are nonsensical. I can own having a lot of internalized random rankings of others, for example people who get up earlier are better than those who sleep later (wonder where I got that one); people who are active are superior to those who aren't; and people who know a lot are more valuable than those who don't. These are all one hundred percent false, of course, but I still notice those biases leaking out from time to time. Once again, awareness is the key. Noticing when you are judging someone or something as wrong, weird, less-than, incorrect, evil, stupid or any other negative label, is the first step. Getting curious about what ideas lie behind that judgment and what needs, desires or values lie behind it that give you back your power and helps you learn more about who you are, what you want and value and what, if anything, you might want to do about it.

Fear as Teacher

Saying *yes* to that which resonates (or to whom you envy) can lead you down wonderful and magical paths, to places you didn't imagine you would ever or could ever go. Learning more about who and what is within you is like taking yourself on a real-life treasure hunt. My experiences up to this point have far outweighed the imaginings of my younger self of what was possible in this world, simply because I learned how to follow and say yes to the resonance. I have traveled to beautiful and interesting places; I have met fascinating people; and I have pursued and experienced many and varied avenues of creativity and self-expression.

Don't get me wrong, it's not always simple or easy to tell when there is resonance. It can be hard to discern the difference between fear or resistance and something that simply doesn't resonate. Fear very often gets in the way and muddies our perception. It can be difficult to distinguish past trauma from a very legitimate warning for the present. My fear of intimacy is a perfectly good example of this, it has had me trying to run from my relationship with my soul mate partner for decades. Fear of intimacy is absolutely a core terror for so many but there are also many other fears that can cause us to shrink. Fear of making the *wrong* decision or fear of being humiliated are big ones. We risk making ugly sounds, bad art, or shitty first drafts; we risk looking ridiculous or scary when we dare to explore our authenticity. We risk falling off the horse or failing spectacularly. I have experienced (and survived) all of this and so much more.

Your Authentic Self isn't perfect, and your authenticity can be messy, vulnerable and yes, sometimes very scary. While we might want to avoid our fear, that fear can actually be worked with, it can be interrogated for information. Fear's purpose is to keep us safe, therefore fear can stop us and prevent our evolution if we don't address it. It is paramount that we find out what is truly behind the fear because left unchecked, fear can create enough resistance that we feel as though it's simply not worth it to try to move forward.

I believe that we are culturally taught to fear our fears. We are taught to run from our fear, believing that being in fear means that we are weak. The contrary is actually true; it takes a tremendous amount of courage to look our fear in the face and even more to give it a voice. Pushing aside our fears doesn't make them go away, in fact it can make them louder in their attempts to get our attention. Our fears have important things to say and there is tremendous power in listening and giving a name to our worst fears. It can be incredibly liberating, like turning on the light and finally looking in the closet, when we get to see that what is actually there is not a monster but instead an idea, a belief, a thought of what we don't want (which tells us what we do, in fact, want). You don't have to share your fears with anyone but yourself but taking the risk and being vulnerable with someone else can yield great rewards in intimacy, connection, and finding allies and support.

Behind every fear exists a legitimate idea, a legitimate desire, making it a tremendously valuable source of insight. When we get this level of clarity and perspective the fear usually lifts, or we are able to walk forward holding fear's hand.

Learning about what's real in you can be a pretty scary prospect so where do we find the courage to pursue our true and Authentic Selves? Once we have felt and recognized these uplifting experiences of resonance and alignment, we can experience a renewed zest and love for ourselves and for life. I have often felt like the lead in a really good love story, willing to slay dragons and go on daring adventures all for the love of my Authentic Self. The writing of this book has been a similar journey; it has had me facing fears, old demons and limiting beliefs in order to fulfill my passionate desire to get at what is in here and put it out into the world.

Recognizing your own uniqueness and tuning into the clues that are alerting you to what is and isn't in alignment with you can indeed be fraught, but it is also amazing, rewarding, fulfilling, satisfying and joyful. Your being is worthy of this exploration and it will reward your efforts with the deep soul satisfaction for which you have been searching.

Authenticity Applied – We Dreamed of the West

From 2000 to 2005 we lived in Annapolis, Maryland. We lived in a beautiful home, in a beautiful neighborhood, close to the charming downtown area. By all accounts this was the dream. The life we had created there looked perfect on paper, but we had a nagging feeling that it wasn't, we just weren't sure yet why.

In 2004 my husband's father was dying and we (middle-agers that we were) started to rethink our lives. Did my husband want to commute two hours each day to work for corporate America? Did we want to keep trying for the bigger house, the better car? What would we like instead? The answer didn't come until we were on a trip out west. Driving west from Lake Tahoe to San Francisco, it hit me like a charging bison, "We belong in the west!" The next summer we packed our kids into our motor home and headed out to explore Wyoming and Montana (because that's what *the west* was to me). I remember standing on the shores of Jenny Lake in Grand Teton National Forest, thinking, "This is what I want, this beauty, this nature!" I just knew I didn't want to be so far from a big city. That night we sat under the stars in Yellowstone National Park and made a wish list of everything we wanted in our new place. We went back to Annapolis, started searching and together with divine providence we found just what we were looking for, a place that checked every box on our wish list. The synchronicity that led us to our new home was off the charts, right down to a free airplane ticket showing up in the mail the day after my husband put out a prayer.

It was a terribly exciting and nerve-wracking time. The urgings were strong, but we also wondered if we were crazy to be making such a big move to a place where we knew not one soul. Some people didn't understand when we told them we were leaving Annapolis. "Why do you want to take your kids away from their school, away from their friends and family?" Yeah, it did sound a little nutty and a little bit selfish. But other people responded with, "Yeah, I totally get it. I wish I was that brave." Ultimately it didn't matter what others said because we needed to listen to our beings, work through our own fears (and there were plenty), take the leap of faith and go west. We definitely had our share of challenges there, but we had many more incredible experiences and we never once doubted our decision.

It's All About You

This exploration is for you. Ultimately you are the authority, you are the author of your own life. People have been saying and will continue to try to say, to define, who and what you are. People will have preferences for how you should be. Some of what you discover will please them, some of what you discover will challenge them. Holding this exploration as an experiment you are conducting, out on a research field trip, or a fact-finding mission can take some of the seriousness or drama out of it, thereby reducing the fear, intimidation, and resistance. At the end of the day this is about your relationship with and your commitment to yourself.

Learning things about yourself can have you running down the road, thinking you know what they mean, believing it is the most significant discovery since the Dead Sea Scrolls. I definitely have a tendency to believe that every person with whom I feel a deep connection will be in my life forever and that every talent I uncover will make me famous. It is hard to know where any of it will lead but have fun, get curious. Here are some questions to help open up your curiosity and exploration. Imagine you get to interview your favorite person on the planet. These are some of the questions you might want to ask.

Exploration and Inquiry

There are no right or wrong answers to these questions, and there will be no grades or exams to follow. You are simply being invited to look more closely at what is in you, to mine all of the nooks and crannies for the gems and treasures that exist within you. I feel excited about what you will discover.

Spotting Resonance:
Think back to a time when you felt really alive, when you were feeling joy, excitement, or awe.
What was happening?
What were you doing?
Who was with you?
What are some adjectives to describe the experience, for example: elated, expansive, comforted?
What did you feel in your body: chills, goosebumps, electricity?
Tuning into what resonance looks and feels like in you, physically, mentally, and emotionally, what else can you add to these memories?
(Remind yourself of the notion of finding experiences when you were sober and if that is not possible trying to separate out what part of that was genuine and not chemically induced.)

Think back to a time when you felt at peace. What was happening?

Think back to a time when things really worked out well, when things flowed or unfolded in a better way than you imagined. What factors contributed?

Think back to a time when you felt anything was possible, to a time when you felt you could do anything.

When was the last time you felt that your heart was open?

Make a list of people, places, things and ideas in your life that you already know you love?
Note how you feel writing that list.

When you were young:
What did you use to love as a child?
How did you use to play as a child?
What did you want to be when you grew up?
What were you encouraged to do or be?
In what ways did you feel free to express yourself?
What kinds of things were encouraged or simply not resisted?

Side note: "What do you want to be when you grow up?" I had answers for that question when I was little but as I got older, I simply grew unsure and uncomfortable with being asked. I didn't have a good answer anymore. I didn't have an answer that I thought would be met with approval by the asker and as a result, I was terribly envious of those people who seemed to have it all figured out. They proclaimed their goal in high school or college and did what they needed to do to make it their career. It seemed so simple. I was all over the board in college, studying biology, art, psychology and social work. I never completed my bachelor's degree because I wasn't passionate about any of it. Apparently, my being wanted to take a long and winding path to my vocation. And guess what? It all makes sense now. I needed to have all of those experiences and I needed all of that education to become who I am today. Yes, I have felt deeply embarrassed that I didn't have a neat and tidy degree and title but today I have the utmost respect and appreciation for myself and the way my life and learning have unfolded.

Your Life Today

When, where, and with whom are you having the most fun.
Around whom do you feel like your best self?
Of whom are you jealous or envious?
Do you have fantasies or daydreams? What about?
What is the deepest desire behind those fantasies or daydreams?
What do you enthusiastically say "Yes" to?

What makes you come to life?
What makes you feel inspired?
What makes you feel awe?
How do you like to move your body?
Where in your life do you feel uninhibited?
Where does your attention regularly go during the day?
To which groups do you belong?
To which groups would you never belong?

In great detail, write or talk about someone whom you greatly admire. Once you have done this answer:
1) Which aspect of this person's being (physical, personality, life circumstances, for example) do you envy or wish you could embody?
2) Where can you find these qualities in your own being/life (no matter how small)?

Recognizing Fear and Resistance:

What are your regular fear stories?
Where did they come from?
How do you become aware of fear? What do you notice?
How do you become aware of resistance? What do you notice?
How do fear and resistance manifest in your mind and/or body?
What do you feel in your body?
Where do you feel it in your body?
What stories are you telling yourself?
What are your "worst case" scenarios?
What kinds of activities did you resist and/or resent in the past?
What kinds of activities do you resist and/or resent now?
How do fear and/or resistance interfere with your path forward?

If you want to awaken all of humanity, then awaken all of yourself.

If you want to eliminate the suffering in the world, then eliminate all that is dark and negative in yourself.

Truly, the greatest gift you have to give is that of your own self-transformation.

- Lao Tzu

SECTION II – Part 2: The False You

If living in alignment with your Authentic Self makes you feel alive, gives you energy and brings joy to your soul, does feeling low energy, lackluster, or depressed mean that you are not living in alignment with your Authentic Self? I believe the short answer to that question is *Yes*. I understand that there are infinite potential explanations or diagnoses for why we might be feeling less than vibrant, but it is my belief that the root cause of this dis-ease, whether it be physical, mental, emotional or spiritual, is simply a life force that isn't able to flow as it should or could. A being who isn't expressing themselves fully is not as alive as they could be*. A being who is not as alive as they could be, will not be living as bright of a life as they could. Thankfully, the blocks that impede this pure energy, this full authentic expression, are detectible. They reside inside and there are many ways to discover/uncover these roots, these thoughts and beliefs, and replace them with the truth. It is possible to recognize that one has been operating from limiting ideas and to then begin to live from a more expanded, more alive place.

Just as with an old house that was originally built with gorgeous wood floors, doors and trim but has been painted and carpeted over multiple times during the years it has been in existence; the fact that this wood has been covered up doesn't negate the fact that the underlying wood still exists and is still gorgeous and solid. Your gorgeous and solid self still exists underneath all of those ideas about who you are and how you should be in the world. Your Authentic Self still lives on despite those layers of falsehood.

*I don't pretend to know what is possible for you or what you need to go through on your journey. If you are dealing with a chronic and/or serious illness you may or may not know that the roots of such an illness are likely very deep. Change is possible and healing is possible, but I don't know what that is meant to look like for you. It might mean reaching the end of the illness and being restored to full health or it might mean improving your outlook or situation while you coexist with the illness. Either way, helping your life force to flow is the most beneficial and loving thing you can do for yourself.

Grab Your Headlamp

Just by existing in the world, we get all kinds of ideas and expectations thrown at us, about how we're meant to behave and what we're supposed to do with our lives. Sadly, we are generally presented with a very narrow range of acceptable parameters and those parameters don't take into consideration the infinite possibilities of how people can actually show up and what they can do with their lives.

Women in the 1950s who wanted to do something other than homemaking and motherhood needed to fight for a different experience or set their dreams aside. Men in the 1960s who wanted to dance, or decorate, or style hair were ridiculed and encouraged to pursue something more masculine. Senior citizens in the 1970s were encouraged to slow down and quietly wait for the end.

Today, while we still have a long way to go, women are working in every arena where the men were prized; gender expectations have become much more open and fluid; and I know 70-year-olds who could literally run circles around a 50-year-old from the past.

Side note: Let's be clear, we are talking about the beliefs that prevent us from living and expressing our full authentic selves. We also absorbed (hopefully) many positive ideas about ourselves and the world, ideas that support our full expression. Those are helpful to recognize and celebrate as fortification against the limiting ones, though, positive messages, when held too fast, can be just as limiting. Do you need to constantly be the nice guy when you aren't feeling nice in the moment, or the smart one when you don't have all of the answers?

The ideas we learned about who we are and how the world operates live in our beings and influence our experiences. In fact, they have been in our beings since they arrived on the scene and weren't challenged, and these *core beliefs* will continue to influence us until they are addressed. Until they are changed, these beliefs are essentially our operating systems. For example, my core belief that I would be criticized or humiliated if I was seen or heard had me unconsciously working hard at keeping myself invisible. That propensity was directly at odds with my desire to be a performer, making it much harder than it needed to be to actually get myself on stage and to let my voice be heard.

Your entire life you have been given or have formed beliefs about yourself: about your appearance, about your personality, about your abilities, and about your potential. You were given, or formed, beliefs about others: about who others are, about their relationship to you, about what they should look like, and about what they are capable of. You learned ideas, as well, about the world and what is possible there. You learned, took in, and formed 360 degrees of ideas, making up the whole of you - just not the *real* you.

We can find and address these ideas by getting curious about which ones we may have learned during our lives. Simply looking at your original family dynamics will tell you so much about what was and wasn't acceptable and about what was believed to be possible or impossible. Who was the boss and what did they tell you?

We can look at our lives as they are now and imagine which beliefs would need to be on board in order to have created that current reality. For example, if I continually fret about money, I surely hold some ideas about money, about how much there is and how much I am allowed to have.

We can also get curious about which ideas are being activated in the moment, when we are triggered. Do you have expectations about how people should show up in relation to you? Do you have beliefs about how good life can or can't be? I often hear people say things like, "Figures!" or "Of course!" when something goes awry. What could that be telling you?

Finding old beliefs and replacing them isn't simply a mental exercise. We are looking for where those beliefs actually live in our bodies, in our past, and in our psyches. It might take some exploration, but once we find those falsehoods, we can replace them with what is actually the truth of who we are.

Side note: If this kind of inquiry feels less fun and you find yourself heading for the exit, I understand. It makes total sense. I would like to offer my encouragement, though, and my hope that you keep going as the payoff is well worth the discomfort.

Authenticity Applied – A Heavy Burden

I was in a place in my life where I felt like I needed to contribute more to our family's financial situation, but I was experiencing a lot of resistance from within. I was certainly willing, but I just couldn't get myself to take any action. I was working with a life coach at the time, so I brought this up in our next session. We talked around the subject for a little bit and I marveled at her own enthusiasm for *work*, she joyfully said she had so many ideas of what she could do next, if coaching didn't work out. I had been a stay-at-home mom for years and had worked a few light coffee shop jobs, which I loved, but I felt ready for something a little meatier. I just felt so heavy every time I considered going out and getting a *job*. My coach asked me to tune into that heaviness in my body, pretty soon I had this image of me struggling under the weight of a man's heavy trench coat and I instantly knew what that was about. My father was very serious about work, he took his responsibility to provide for our family to heart. In his mind, working and providing were very serious and heavy burdens he bore for our family. With that clarity, in my mind's eye, I imagined myself standing upright, taking off that coat and handing it back to my father, with my love and appreciation for all he had done for us. I, however, was daring to imagine that my contribution to providing for our family could be a lighter, more joyful experience. I started to dream up what kind of job I was qualified for and that I would actually have fun doing. Once taking action was no longer a hurdle, I found that job, loved it and kept it until it was time for something different.

Awareness and Inquiry

Just as when we are seeking the light that lives within, searching in the shadows for the limiting beliefs requires awareness. If the opposite of resonance is dissonance, discerning what dissonance feels like in your being is a great place to start to build awareness. What does it feel like when things aren't quite right, when they are not in alignment? Does it feel like heaviness, sluggishness, tension, or nausea in your body? Do you have tightness in your chest? Does your head hurt, or do you feel lightheaded? Do you suddenly feel tense and resistant or sleepy, perhaps? Do you feel confused or does your mind go blank? Your being knows what's up and it does its best to communicate that information to you, it's simply your job to learn to become aware, to recognize and to decipher the clues.

Our beings know what is true and they want us to have this information. That information is alive and well somewhere within you. Your being (and your own spiritual support squad) is working with you to bring it forward, but there is more you can do to discover what goes on inside, to find which ideas are taking up residence in your being.

What Were You Taught:
About yourself – Your body, your personality, your psychology, your abilities, your potential, and your future?
About others – Relationships, family, support, expectations, safety?
About humanity – Who are we as humans? Why are we here?
About society – Government, culture, services, work?
About the world – Is it a safe place? What is possible here? What isn't possible here?
About spirituality – A higher power, support, what you should and shouldn't do. What happens when you do or don't do those things? What should other people do or not do?

In what ways were you censored?
What didn't feel possible because of familial or societal expectations?
What wasn't acceptable in your world, especially in your family?

How does that still show up today? We often continue the message in the absence of our caregivers.

What Did You Learn:
About dreams?
About talents?
About desires?
About attractions?
About duties and obligations?

Look at your life as it is today for signs and clues as to how you might be out of alignment.

In which areas of your life are you experiencing dissonance?
Do you spend your time working at a job you hate?
Are you finding yourself wanting more meaning in your life?
Are you in the habit of stirring up trouble?
Does life itself feel like it is f-ing with you?
Are challenging relationships the norm for you?
Does it feel like you are regularly in search of something you can't quite name?
Do you feel like you keep heading toward a goal only to have your efforts derailed or do you derail them yourself?

Caution: It can be easy to read the preceding questions and determine that all is not well in your world. If that is happening, please pause, take a deep breath, and reread *What I Want You to Know* and *What Else*. You can take your time with these changes, little by little. Remember it is a process. Mostly I want you to believe that it is possible to create a different reality for yourself and your life.

More Inquiry
Look at the circumstances in your life that you wish were different.
Ask yourself: What would I have to believe in order to create this scenario?
Notice about what or whom you regularly complain. Why?
What complaints do you imagine others have about you?
What complaints do you know others have about you?
What are your pet peeves?
What labels do you use to describe yourself?
To which groups (formal or informal) would you never want to belong?

Write or talk about, in great detail, someone you have little tolerance for. Then answer:
1) What needs, desires, and dreams are activated here?
2) Find where those abhorrent qualities live in you.
3) What did you learn about why those qualities were so abhorrent?
4) How might those qualities actually be strengths?

Judgments – Take Two

Once again, judgments can be helpful in showing us what we learned and what we believe about ourselves, others and the world. What are some of your strong judgments? What are they telling you? If you grew up in a household with strong beliefs and messages, of any kind, those ideas likely stuck and can absolutely impede your life force and expression. Here's one of my judgments that surfaces whenever a big pickup truck comes up quickly and closely behind me on the highway, especially when I am passing another vehicle. My kneejerk reaction is to judge that person as rude, aggressive and probably a white conservative man. What is this telling me? That I don't feel respected and I want to feel respected; that I don't feel safe and I want to feel safe. That is not their job, that is my job. Yes, I would prefer it if people didn't drive aggressively but it's better for me to focus on what is alive in me in that moment. It's better for me to look for old ideas that are getting activated than try to change someone else's behavior (especially since I have no control over a stranger in a passing truck). What I discover when I inquire more deeply is that while my father didn't drive a big pickup truck, he was a traditional conservative man and he was pretty aggressive with his desires and opinions, impatiently running mine right over. I believed that what I wanted and what I thought was less important. While it might have felt that way growing up, it is definitely not true today. I get to take up space, I get to be heard and if someone doesn't like it that is for them to attend to.

Regarding Dreams

The topic of dreams can be complex and emotionally charged, calling to mind limiting ideas such as: dreams are dangerous; dreams don't come true; no one would support my dreams. I was an imaginative dreamer when I was younger, but I had no idea and very little guidance about how to actually make those dreams come true. I could see the dreams very clearly, but they existed on an island, far from the shore on which I was standing. The only strategy I had then was to pray for a miracle (since I didn't think a magic lamp was likely to drop in my lap, though I really, really wished one would). I did not get a lot of messaging that dreaming was worthwhile or fruitful, but because I have learned over time to listen to and trust in my dreams I have so much more faith in them and their value for helping me see what is within and in which direction to head. In fact, I can be fairly audacious now with the size of my dreams, as you will see later on in the book. Interrogating what you learned about dreaming can reveal hidden beliefs and hidden gems.

Was dreaming encouraged and/or allowed in your household?
What was possible?
Who was allowed to dream?
Which dreams did you have?
Which dreams did you put aside?
Which dreams seemed impossible then?
Which dreams seem impossible now?
What dreams do you dare to have today?
What would you need to believe in order to make them come true?

Authenticity Applied – We Really Do Know

My oldest sister took horseback riding lessons for a little while when I was very young, and from my first moment of seeing a horse I was hooked, obsessed, and horse crazy. Anything to do with horses, from the pictures in my sister's horse book to her ceramic horse figurines would elicit my passion. I wanted a horse. Bad. I wanted riding lessons. Desperately. I wanted to look at the horse book and dream of which horse I would someday own. It was always a toss-up between the Paint and the Palomino.

My parents couldn't afford lessons or a horse for me and no amount of whining, fussing or crying could change that reality. I had to settle for drawing pictures of them and riding my bike to a nearby pasture to look at them. It wasn't until I was an adult with my own paycheck that I realized I could make my dream of riding horses a reality. My inner five-year-old self was grinning from ear to ear. I was finally able to groom, ride, and develop relationships with these magnificent creatures with whom I had felt a kinship for most of my life. Even though sometimes I can still feel a little nervous around them, my affinity for them has never waned, and I have never not wanted to have horses in my life. My five-year-old self definitely knew what she wanted.

The Meat of the Moment

Once in a while (or perhaps more frequently than you would like) things unravel in the moment. Something triggers an emotional response in you, and you've lost your perspective and your connection to your center. Not much can be done until you are able to recognize that you are triggered. Once you gain the awareness that you are in a stress response, in a state of nervous system dysregulation, you can begin to get back on track. Pause. Breathe. Reflect. Get curious about what is going on inside. What happened? What did you hear, feel, or think that caused this reaction?

Here is an example of one way to process when you find yourself bumping up against fear, resistance, or an obvious block. Either in that moment or when you are able to be alone and quiet, ask yourself these questions. Also note, when you are trying to uncover a core belief it can be helpful to try out a few different possibilities and a few different ideas, to see which one really resonates. The idea might be, "I am unlovable" or it might be, "I am not important". They're similar but different. Your being knows and will let you know when you've landed on the one that feels true.

What are you feeling emotionally or physically, right now?
Where do you feel it in your body?
Can you ask yourself to go back to a time when you first felt this way?
What was happening?
What belief or beliefs did you form about yourself, others, or the world from this experience?
Challenge this idea, reality check it. (Core beliefs tend to be absolute.)
Is this universally true, can you find exceptions?
What new belief would you like to live by instead?
Imagine what it would be like to live by this new belief.
What would it make possible in your life?

The same practitioners and practices (found on page 56) that we employ to discover the gems inside are great aids in this shadow discovery work as well. Any modality that can put you more in touch with what is happening in your psyche and your body is beneficial. Any practitioner, with whom you feel safe showing up as you are, will be able to help encourage these ideas to come to the surface.

Modalities for Discovering and Healing Limiting Beliefs:

Psychotherapy
Massage
Yoga
Trauma informed yoga
Reiki
Cranio-sacral therapy
Acupuncture
Chiropractic adjustments
Core Belief work
Ho'oponopono
Radical Forgiveness
Psychedelic therapy
The Feldenkrais Method
Rolfing
Therapeutic touch
Somatic therapies
Akashic Record readings

In short, the most important elements for dealing with limiting core beliefs are the ability to:
- Cultivate awareness about what you're feeling and when.
- Get curious about the present dynamics and the past learning.
- Separate from the old message by asking, "what would I have to believe about myself, others or the world for this to be playing out currently?"
- Acknowledge this information/insight and perhaps share it with another safe person.
- Identify what is actually true.

As I said, unearthing these limiting core beliefs is a long game but one that is totally worth it. I have transformed myself from a shy, nervous person with no voice to one who dares to believe that she has something worth sharing with the world.

Just Let Me Fix It

One last little tool for glimpsing limiting beliefs is looking at what you're dying to *fix*. Wanting to change the things in your world that you don't like is normal. Wanting to fix the things that we perceive as wrong, to try to do whatever is in our power to restore things to the way we think they should be, is natural. This is human nature and since most of us are thusly inclined we can use this desire as an opportunity to, once again, learn more about ourselves and what we believe.

What do you find yourself trying to fix?

    In yourself – with your body, your personality, your habits

    In your relationships – with how others show up

    In your environment – with physical aspects, energy

    In the world – with people, politics, planet

What might you be trying to accomplish? What needs/desires are you trying to fulfill? What is the source of your discomfort with the way things are? There will likely be an answer that is tied to some limiting idea that you hold. For example, my attempts to *fix* my posture are partially driven by vanity, I just don't think it *looks good*. And then there is always another deeper, more authentic need or desire, which in the case of my posture is the desire for a healthy, aligned spine. I find myself wanting to *fix* relationships because I dislike conflict but also because I have a sincere and abiding desire for the flow of love to be restored.

Understanding what drives this desire to change things is crucial. Many of the things which we are trying to *fix* are not actually within our power to change, it also might not be our place to determine whether or not they should be changed. That is important to realize, but the reasons *behind* the desire to fix are the most important bits of awareness for you. Once you get to the understanding of which needs/desires you are trying to meet/fulfill, you can adjust things within your own being. The power will be restored to its proper place and you won't necessarily need anything outside of you to change for peace to be experienced. You get to hear and understand what you want and need. You then get to do something about it. These are your valuable clues for tending to yourself.

Go with Care

Should you choose to delve into this inner exploration, I urge you, again, to be gentle; this is no place for shame, blame, or unrealistic expectations. Remember, it can be scary because these old ideas were instilled in order to help keep you safe. You get to choose which ones to address and how quickly or slowly you work. I encourage you, if you have the resources, to find a practitioner with whom you can partner in this inner work. Someone who has experience and can be objective and separated from the dramas or traumas in your life. Finding support in the absence of financial resources is absolutely possible and could look like journaling, talking with safe friends, finding out which free services are available in your community, checking out self-help books from the library, watching videos, or following social media channels that deal with mental health, core beliefs, self-discovery, or authenticity.

Once you bring these false and limiting ideas to consciousness, and replace them with the actual truth, you get to have a new and different experience of yourself and of life. You will stop seeing certain dynamics repeat themselves. You will have even more courage to head in the direction of your dreams and you will feel like you are capable of actually making those dreams come true. The underlying story about who you are and what you can do will be rewritten, having the ending you want to see.

Everything changes when you start to emit your own frequency rather than absorbing the frequencies around you. When you start imprinting your intent on the universe rather than receiving an imprint from existence.

- Barbara Marciniak

SECTION III: Your Best Self

We are all just trying to be okay, every one of us, every day. It's my belief that we are all, in some way, trying to numb or blot out the pain of the wounds we have received during our lives, as well as the pain of not living our Authentic Selves. We are trying to find strategies to help us feel happiness or joy through chemicals, media, or the relationship game, but often we are left feeling disappointed, depressed, or disillusioned when the desired effect falls flat or doesn't last. These temporary, inauthentic (though often quite valid and necessary at the time) remedies, can also lose their potency over time or be taken away as they exist outside of us; when you have to stop drinking, when the soul mate leaves, or when your phone dies. Anchoring into the magic that lives within you means that you are connected to something that endures, and simply cannot be taken away (only temporarily forgotten).

In my experience, nothing can beat the feeling of living and expressing my Authentic Self, not money, not religion, not alcohol, not finding a guru or a soul mate, not even finding my *purpose*. I have been on this path of self-discovery and spirituality my whole adult life. This has been my quest, my holy grail, and I have spent many of those years looking outside of myself for this bliss - from alcohol, to men, to shopping, to spirituality, to dreams on the horizon. I have been down, depressed and not wanted to continue on with life and this is the only focus that has consistently pulled me through; this is what my soul has been searching for, as is everyone's, I believe. This pursuit is my soul's true mission.

Your Best Life

The benefits of living your Authentic Self are many, varied and abundant and they include every part of your being. By living and expressing your authenticity you literally make (and continue to make) your life the best it can be, and your impact on the world is just as potent. In that context, I can't think of a more valuable pursuit. The actual dreaming up and writing of this book has been the most fun, and I am honored, blessed and ecstatic to be doing it. Those blessings will continue to reverberate throughout my body, my mind and my spirit long after I have finished writing it.

True joy is a natural byproduct of connecting with your Authentic Self – that uplifting feeling that accompanies being on target and in alignment. We can, as I have said over and over, find what brings us joy but many of us have been taught to minimize the actual value of joy. It's nice when it comes along, but our culture tends to value work, doing, and achieving, above all else. Joy can also feel weird and unfamiliar if things in our lives have been rough. Our culture certainly talks about valuing love, as well as joy, but did you know that according to the late Dr. David Hawkins (psychiatrist, spiritual teacher and author of *Power vs Force*), joy has a higher vibrational frequency than love? Through muscle testing (aka applied kinesiology) Hawkins calibrated the vibrational frequencies of our human emotions and experiences with a scale ranging from twenty (shame) to one thousand (enlightenment). It's easy to see, for example, how courage (which vibrates at 200) might be considered a more desirable or valuable emotion than shame (which vibrates at 20), and if we were to approach joy versus love simply in these terms, joy – being higher up on the vibrational scale at 540 would be a more valuable emotion than love vibrating at 500. We could make it a higher priority to seek or cultivate joy than to seek love. That is certainly not how most of us were taught to think. Seeking joy sounds a lot like "seeking pleasure" which can be seen through the lenses of selfishness and/or hedonism. It can look or sound like a shallow pursuit when the truth, however, is that we were made to feel joy, it is our birthright and seeking it is a completely valid, worthwhile, and enlightened pursuit.

In addition to joy, we get to experience actual peace when we are living in alignment with ourselves. Through living in alignment, our beings are able to release a lot of the tension associated with suppressed expression and the searching/seeking that can accompany a fraught existence. Dr. Hawkins asserts that peace calibrates at 600 on his scale, an even higher frequency than that of joy. Peace tells us we have arrived at a place of not trying, a place of harmony where things are as they should be. Peace can also be an undervalued experience in our competitive world, though it is obvious to most of us that we could all use a little more peace.

Recognizing that experiencing one's Authentic Self brings joy and peace means that you can safely and confidently point your compass heading in that direction. No matter what else you are doing with your life, if you are focused on your authentic expression you are on course to a brighter existence.

Your Joy Is Contagious

Your joyful creative expression matters. When you are creating and resonating with joy and peace it impacts not just you and your life, enabling you to continue to up-level your life, to make better and better choices, and to have more and more amazing experiences, but this also has a tremendously positive practical and energetic impact on the rest of the world.

Your being, no matter which state it is in, is contagious. When it is in a state of joy and/or peace, it has much more to offer the world. The short story is that we respond to environmental vibrational frequencies, mostly unconsciously, and our frequencies impact others as well. Living a life with less stress is significant, living a life with more joy and/or peace is transformational for everyone. When we're living our best lives, the impact on the others in our lives can't help but be positive. If you need any more convincing, simply think about the impact you can have on others when you are miserable. It truly is in the best interest of all for us to be living our Authentic Selves.

When you are in alignment with yourself you simply become a better person because that is the truth of who you are, and makes it much more difficult to see others as less than or separate from you. A happy and fulfilled person is a kind, generous, and forgiving person to others. The knowledge of who I am, this consciousness of love at my core, is what has had the biggest impact on the kind of person I am able to be in the world. I am more accepting and more compassionate than I have ever been, and it wasn't the *shoulds* that I was taught in my religious upbringing that truly allowed me to organically show up this way. True kindness and empathy flow freely and naturally from an expansive and regulated state.

Better Health is Wealth

When you are aligned with yourself, when you are not struggling, fighting, or resisting, every aspect of your being is in better health. When you are experiencing harmony in your being, your nervous system is allowed the opportunity to come back online and regulate. When your nervous system is regulated you have more energy and focus for other things. Your being is not in a state of fight, flight, freeze or fawn, meaning you have better access to rational and, maybe more importantly, creative thought.

Most illness and disease are connected to stress, this is well documented. The toll that being in a state of dysregulation takes on your being is profound. It stands to reason then, that to live in more peace, more ease and more joy – to live with your life force freely flowing through your body – would lead to overall better health. Your mind is clearer and more balanced; your emotions are better able to move through you and find balance and harmony; you are better connected to your needs, desires, hopes and dreams and you are better equipped to meet those needs, desires, hopes and dreams.

Authentic Connection

Recognizing and connecting with your Authentic Self and the Authentic Selves of others in your life goes a long way toward fostering intimacy and connection. It creates a lovely level of mutual safety which is needed for intimacy and connection to occur. On some level, people recognize through which lens they are being perceived and when you hold the divine truth about another, when you are able to recognize that there is more to them than meets the eye, they're going to feel it.

Knowing who you are makes you less vulnerable to the judgments and reactions of others. When we are connected to and aware of what is going on within ourselves emotionally, when in relationship with another, we are better able to separate out which are our triggers and which are not, what is our responsibility and what is not.

Recognizing, owning and tending to the experiences we are having within ourselves helps reduce drama and conflict with others. When you know what is true and alive in yourself and can take care of your feelings and needs, your feelings get to have the attention they need and deserve from you. You are also able to take the focus off of the perceived wrong doer, helping that person relax and focus on their own inner world. Your relationships can enjoy less tension because you are no longer putting undue pressure on those outside of yourself to be responsible for the wounds and holes that need to be tended to and filled by you. This frees you both to be more willing and available to support each other as needed.

In my experience, the most wonderful impact of authenticity on our relationships with others is the intimacy, connection, and magic made possible when we are simply able to show up as our Authentic Selves. And when we are able to show up authentically, the more others will feel able to do the same. There are no filters, no barriers to simply being able to see and be seen. And when we purely see and are purely seen we get to experience the presence of the divine.

What Doesn't Fit

Another subtle and beautiful blessing I have noticed is that things that are not in alignment with the Authentic Self will either not come into your life or will usually leave your life naturally and easily because they simply do not fit. Things, ideas and people that don't resonate will just obviously no longer belong in your life. Disclaimer: It is not quite as simple with people who have been in our lives for a while. We can tend to want to hold on to people who no longer resonate or give the boot to people who merely challenge us but actually do resonate. There appears to be a popular attitude encouraging people to get rid of those with whom we have challenges, but I suggest that being challenged isn't necessarily the same as being out of alignment with someone. These people can act as powerful teachers when we are willing and able to view them as such. Recognizing that people can change, grow, evolve, shift and make their way into a more harmonious frequency can make them seem less disposable and more like partners and collaborators on the journey. People who have no interest in changing or growing, however, simply won't fit long-term in relationship with someone who is intentionally evolving.

Authenticity Applied - Shame

The more you live by the things that are real and true to your soul, the less important things like what size you are, how much money you make or what others think about all of that, will seem. The less shame you will feel and the more you will feel at peace with your authentic life as it is.

One day, when my kids were young and in school, I was on the phone with a bankruptcy lawyer. At that very moment one of my kids came into the room and told me she found out at school that she had lice. I remember thinking in that next moment, "Lice and filing for bankruptcy, all on the same day! Two things that in the past would have caused me so much shame, and today I'm okay!" What a liberating awareness. I wasn't thrilled about either of them, but I didn't have to add shame and embarrassment to my list of things to deal with, all because I had been doing the work of releasing those old ideas and building trust in how my life was unfolding.

A Brilliant Mirror

All of the benefits that I lay out above would seem like enough of a payoff right there for practicing authenticity, but it thrills me to no end to know that this brilliance of which I speak is in each person I encounter and that knowledge has a profoundly healing impact on me and, equally important, a profoundly healing impact on whomever I encounter. When this is what you see when you look at another, you both have the opportunity to have that mirror image come to life in them; their being awakens with that recognition. You literally, with just a knowing smile, can change someone's world. This is actually how healers heal. They see the truth about who a person is and the potential for being restored to their true essence is brought to reality.

Knowing that we are contributing to the world, and that we have value - that we matter, gives meaning to our lives. It gives us another reason to get out of bed in the morning. Knowing that who we are, just by being ourselves, contributes to the positivity of the world is possibly 180 degrees from what you were taught about your worth in the world and what you needed to do in order to have worth.

The knowledge of seeing this truth in others makes this journey even more fun and fulfilling. Imagine doing more with this information than simply recognizing it. What would it look like to be active with this kind of knowledge? You might be more of a cheerleader for yourself and for others; you might be more interested in finding out what is in there when you encounter another; you might be more willing to spend the time listening to someone's dreams, ideas, and experiences. Think of all of the important, profound, revolutionary, and soul enriching things that have existed because of someone's authentic expression; because someone was tapped in and brave enough to bring forth their gift for the world, and because someone else listened and supported it. Think of all of the important, profound, revolutionary and soul enriching things that are still waiting to be brought into the world? Truly, what could be more fun?

Don't ask yourself what the world needs, ask yourself what makes you come alive. And then do that. Because what the world needs are people who have come alive.

- Harold Whitman

SECTION IV: Making it Yours

As I have said a few times already, this journey to your Authentic Self is a process and when you claim this path it becomes a practice. It becomes a compass heading for your day and for your life. You are so much more than you have been taught and when you are conscious of what you are doing with your time here you can bring more life to your life. We can all absolutely put authenticity into action and into practice.

Setting the Course

The start of the day. Sunrise. Dawn. Morning. Opening your eyes. Getting out of bed. Stumbling out of bed. Pulling the covers back over your head. The "I can't do anything without my coffee" mantra. People have been talking, writing, and singing about this moment in time for eons. There is a reason for that. It is the most important and most potent point of the day. We joke about it, we lament about it, but it deserves to not be taken lightly. We are coming back to life after the death of sleep. We have been given the opportunity to live another day. And yet most of us disregard its significance by not giving it a second thought once we have opened our eyes and shifted into autopilot. For some it can be the toughest, most excruciating moment of the day. Getting out of bed can be difficult, especially when you don't know why you're doing it. That all can change, and it doesn't need to take hours of meditation to get yourself there. Having some connection (even if it's for just a few minutes) to who you are, what you love and what you're about can set the tone and the compass heading for your day. You might already have a "morning practice" or you might resist the heck out of one. The good news for you is that something as simple as taking a few deep conscious breaths, or tuning into a gratitude, spending time journaling, or simply noticing and enjoying the smell of the coffee as it brews can have the power to set your being on a positive trajectory. You can set your baseline vibe and even if it is short lived, it will build new pathways in your being.

Finding Your Flow

Every day you are faced with choices about which actions to take next. That means that every day you are given opportunities to apply these tools. One of the simplest and easiest ways I *practice* authenticity is by tuning into my to-do list. Sometimes that list is stupidly long, and the act of confronting it can be an overwhelming endeavor in and of itself, but then I settle down and tune into my being. I ask myself which item on that list do I feel the most excited about or the least resistance about and then I do that one first. Then I ask the same question until the tasks are done. That way I am allowing my whole being to be a part of the decision-making process as opposed to merely thinking my way through the list. I simply follow the life, energy, and flow. Maybe you have a lot of resistance to one thing on your list, but your mind is telling you it must be done. By listening to your inner being you might postpone that item, and then learn something that helps you do that task or something that makes the task no longer necessary. Our beings are hooked up and when we listen to them, we are very often helped. This is such an excellent practice for cultivating awareness and for making choices from a place other than a logical one.

Side note: When you resist a particular task to the point of chronic procrastination, ask yourself why. There is usually a very legitimate reason behind that resistance. You're not lazy, you're not a loser, you simply might not feel like you have the information you need. You might not feel like you have the energy to do it. You might fear that you don't have enough time. I found a helpful little tool for the time snag. Time yourself performing the task. Often things we put off or dread take only minutes to actually complete. My husband used to procrastinate mowing the lawn until I timed him, and he discovered that it only took six minutes. From then on it didn't feel so overwhelming to him. Another hack is breaking the task down into bite-sized bits. Every task is made up of many steps, breaking it down into those smaller steps can help make an overwhelming project doable. Our minds are telling us stories all day long, most of which need to be fact checked and rewritten.

Decisions, Decisions

Sometimes, during your day (or life), there is an impasse and you're having trouble deciding in which direction to head. Your mind can paralyze you by convincing you that there is only one right direction, making the other one the wrong one. It isn't usually that black and white, but there might be one that is more in alignment with you and your highest good. Setting that intention for your highest good and then simply taking a step or two in one direction can help you see what unfolds. Again, follow the life and the energy. Follow the one you desire, the one that brings you joy. If it is the direction that is best, things will generally flow and unfold more easily. If it isn't you will be met with obstacles, and things will be bumpy and unclear. If you get new information, it is absolutely reasonable to recalculate your route. When you know who you are and where you are headed, the idea of getting lost isn't as scary because you can trust that the ultimate course has been set. As Dori, from Finding Nemo fame says, "Just keep swimming". Or in my case, when I don't know where my writing is going I "just keep writing". If you continue to follow the flow you will eventually find the path that feels right.

Restoring Balance

Most of us are aware that we live in a culture that values doing, action, and productivity over rest and inner reflection. Home Depot's current tag line is, "Where doers get more done." Be a doer and be cool.

But our beings are designed to have both experiences. In fact, both are necessary. We need balance. Most of us are out of balance, having bought into that Home Depot brand of messaging. Keep doing and you will get everything you want. Instead what you get is burnout. We need rest, we need time to feel, to imagine, to reflect, and to dream - time that isn't filled with endless scrolling, especially if you are working towards living an authentic life. Being quiet and still allows you to listen to all of the wonderful things the still small voice inside has to say.

Some of us, on the other hand, are so weary that we can't get ourselves to stop resting. For whatever reason we don't have the life force to take much action at all. Objectively, this is not necessarily a bad thing, but it can be discouraging, not to mention the guilt and shame of not going along with the societal expectations. What do we need? What do you need? Your being knows. Your being knows and it might not be what your mind is telling you. There was a point in my life when I felt chronically tired. My mind kept telling me I must need more rest but in fact what I needed was a different kind of movement from the busyness I was used to experiencing. I could get myself to hop out of bed and find chores all the live long day and then collapse in an exhausted heap at the end of the day. Instead I needed to mindfully move my body and energy in activities that were not result-oriented but rather were fun, playful, easy. And when I rested, I needed time and space to let my mind wander and dream. We all require action and stillness; outward times and inward times; structure and fluidity; ebb and flow. We have our own seasons and they feed each other. After all, we are nature.

I heard a screenwriter give a talk one time and she said, "Writing can look a lot like lying on the couch or it can look like petting the cat". We need a break from all of the external input so that we can hear what is inside. If I didn't know how to move differently and how to really rest and dream this book would never exist. Learning about what you need throughout your day can take some time, and it can take some reprogramming from ideas you have taken on. Giving yourself the opportunity to play and experiment with different ways of being can open up new doors, inside and out. Incidentally, having fun and playing are very good ways to stimulate creativity and problem solving so make sure they're on the list of possibilities. The more you give yourself permission to have the whole range of experiences, freeing yourself from the expectations of others, the more you will be able to move authentically into whichever experience your being is asking for.

Being with You Now

There is another kind of authentic expression and that has to do with simply coming into awareness and sharing what is alive in you at the moment, i.e. your thoughts, feelings, desires. The Authentic Relating activity, for just this purpose, is called The Noticing Game. It is played with one other person. Once the participants have gotten themselves connected to the present moment (via following their breath or feeling into their seat or feet) one person starts by saying "Being with you now, I notice" and then reports on whatever catches their awareness in that next moment, in that instant. They might notice something they see with their eyes, something they feel in their body, something they feel emotionally or something they're thinking in their head. Then the partner says, "Hearing that, I notice" and reports on whatever they notice in the next moment. It need not be related at all to what the first person said. In fact, this is not a conversation; it is simply a tool for practicing the awareness of what one is experiencing in the moment and then sharing that information with another person. The game continues for a few rounds, going back and forth while continuing to return to what is alive in the next moment. We can all too often get caught up in the thoughts and stories we have in our heads, but they might not actually reflect what our beings or other beings are actually and authentically experiencing. Here we have the opportunity to know ourselves more deeply and we give others the opportunity to know us more deeply as well.

Welcoming Everything

I also learned about the concept of *welcoming everything* during my training with Authentic Relating. I can hear some of you right now. Are you mad?! What about boundaries? What about discernment? I welcome your resistance to this idea, but it is not as radical or scary as it sounds. It simply asks us to take a moment to notice what is happening and to allow it, to refrain from the impulse to resist it or react. Once you make the conscious choice to let whatever is happening in, you have the opportunity to choose what you would like to do with it. Fear and resistance limit our options. They muddle our brains and rob us of our creative problem-solving abilities. When we adopt an *I don't like that* attitude we don't have the space or opportunity to inquire about or understand why we don't like it, or what we would like instead. It doesn't mean we allow unsafe, destructive, or abusive behavior, I am not talking about that (though this practice would make you better able to navigate those scenarios). I am simply suggesting a pause in the moment, a letting go of the tension and resistance and offering an attitude of openness and curiosity. What is this bringing me? What if I didn't have to fight this? I love a good sauna and have learned that the only way for me to endure the discomfort of the heat is to welcome it. To contract or resist the heat only makes the time spent there more difficult to endure.

We have opportunities all day long to resist stories, events, and most especially people. Who in your life do you resist and why? There is a lot to be learned from the answers to those questions, from what exactly you find irritating. I believe we have been taught to resist the unconditional acceptance of others, because we think it gives them permission to slide into slovenly complacency. Somehow, we are taught that it's on us to hold people to a higher standard. At least those are ideas that I took on. We run into trouble when we expect others to behave as we would, when we think they *should* behave as we would. The truth is that when we welcome and accept people as they are, where they are, they are actually able to become even more because that is their true nature. We free them from having to battle yet another person's judgments when we welcome all of who they are.

Intentionally Raising Your Vibration

All of this awareness we have been practicing, this tuning into which experiences uplift, can give you a resource for the future, for when you find you need to shift yourself into a better state. Once you learn which things in your life have a positive impact, you can then begin to use them to consciously raise your own vibration. You can lift yourself out of a funk and not only will you feel better, but you will also be a better problem solver for dealing with what got you into the funk in the first place. As Albert Einstein said, "We cannot solve our problems with the same thinking we used when we created them". Raising your vibration resets your nervous system, clears your head and your energetic field, and gives you access to higher thought and a broader perspective. It can be a brilliant way to start each day.

Fear causes us to contract, to become denser. Fear narrows our focus. When we are in fear, we don't have access to our more expansive ways of thinking. When we use the tool of intentionally raising our vibration, we create more space in our bodies and our minds; we expand our consciousness, giving us access to many more possibilities. Most of us have probably had the experience of being in a downward *spiral*, well, raising your vibration can help you spiral upward. When you move yourself in the direction of higher vibrations you give yourself the opportunity to change things to a trajectory that is continuing to climb. At any moment of awareness, you have the opportunity to lower the vibration, keep it the same or raise it; to put it more simply, at any moment in time we can make things worse, keep them the same or make them better. That power always rests with you.

You can compile your own list of which things bring you to life. You can then fine-tune that list so that you can find just what you're needing in the moment. Which things bring you joy, make you feel relaxed or peaceful, get your blood pumping or your heart to open?

Disclaimer: The use of this list is not intended as a *spiritual bypass*, a term used to describe a way in which we can evade our emotions in an effort to *transcend* them, a way that we can use our larger perspective and understanding to avoid any pain we are feeling because we see the bigger picture. Using *positivity* in this way doesn't move you further along, it simply distracts you for the moment, and you will find those uncomfortable emotions are still waiting for you when you are no longer distracted. Consciously raising your vibration, instead, is a tool for helping you to consciously and deliberately work with and through what is alive and happening with you in the moment.

If and when you notice that you are feeling restless, stuck, numb, agitated, or depressed, congratulations because you had the awareness to notice. The next step is to see which action you would like to take to help shift yourself into a different vibe. You can look at the following list and feel into which action speaks to you in that moment. There are simple, in-the-moment steps or bigger, more time-consuming steps.

Side note: Nature has an inherently high vibration and getting outside in the elements, even if it is simply standing barefoot on a tiny patch of grass, will shift your energy almost immediately.

Add to this list the actions that you already know have the ability to make you feel the way you want to feel:

Pause
Slow everything down
Observe your breathing
Breathe with a 5 second inhalation and a 5 second exhalation
Lift your head and look around at your surroundings
Pray for yourself, for someone else, or for the world
Meditate
Repeat a mantra of your choosing or use your full name as a mantra
Feel into your feet
Stand with your bare feet directly on the earth.
Spend some time in nature and the elements.
Use your senses to experience your outdoor or indoor surroundings
Tidy or clean up your space or an area of your space
Light a candle
Burn incense
Observe or interact with animals/pets
Read something funny or inspiring
Journal
Create art
Start a hobby
Engage in an existing hobby
Listen to music, whichever kind is speaking to you at the moment
Listen to classical music
Sing loudly

Play Solfeggio frequencies
Move your body by walking, cleaning, dancing, yoga, exercise
Have a dance party (either alone or with others, depending on your comfort level)
Smile at yourself or at a stranger
Write a love letter to yourself
Write a letter to someone
Appreciate someone
Make a gratitude list
Help someone
Accept help from someone
Watch funny or inspiring content
Play, either alone or with others
Recreate play you enjoyed as a child
Build something
Restore something
Talk to uplifting friends or relatives
Attend in-person or watch a sporting event
Attend in-person or watch a Live performance

Noticing the Good Stuff

Noticing when things aren't the way we like them to be is important and valid. Most of us have been very well trained in spotting the problem, in finding what doesn't work, where we are limited, and in finding what is broken. We can tend to keep our diagnostic radar trained on that, and it is helpful information to be sure, but it is also critical that we learn to notice what *is* working, what is good, when we are making progress and when things *are* the way we like them. This information is just as valuable. I would argue, actually, that it is more valuable, and it is simply much more fun. There are a million things going right in every moment, and with this intention, you get to spot them.

Grat-i-tude: the quality of being grateful.

Practicing gratitude has gotten quite a lot of airtime in the past few decades. We have heard a lot about it as a tool for what ails you. Just be grateful. As a tool it had lost its luster for me. I had a bit of baggage around it for a while because as a child I was told I *should* be grateful, especially when I would gripe about something. Gratitude actually became a chore, an obligation, it became heavy. In certain mental health circles, "Do your gratitude list" became the remedy for any complaint and elicited guilt whenever I didn't feel grateful. I can still feel resistance today when I feel as though I am expected to be grateful. But gratefulness, genuinely, is a fabulous, uplifting and beneficial tool. Authentic gratitude can't be forced or manufactured, but it can be learned, and it can be practiced. And from a place of freedom, openness and helpfulness, I hope to inspire you to allow gratitude in. There are indeed a million things going right at any given moment, in the world and in your life and nothing is too small to be gratefully noticed. This awareness is not meant as another spiritual bypass idea – where you are meant to feel grateful instead of whatever *negative* feelings you might be feeling. It is simply a healthy practice for instilling more joy, more light, more fun into your life, and for helping you see the brilliant reality of your life, especially in times when it seems there is only darkness.

Cel-e-bra-tion: the action of marking one's pleasure at an important event or occasion by engaging in enjoyable, typically social activity.

I think of celebrating as gratitude turned up a notch and when you practice celebrating, you will soon see it happen spontaneously. You will notice the good stuff, feel grateful and then celebrate. It has an uplifting impact on your being, especially when you share with others the good stuff you notice.

As with most of these concepts, awareness is the key, the first step. What does it look, feel and sound like to notice the good stuff and what do you do with it? Do you find yourself smiling more? Do you have more energy, or a bounce in your step? Maybe you caught yourself releasing a small satisfied sigh. Notice those things and get curious. What is going well? What am I liking right now? How do I feel about that?

Yay is a word I use a lot, as are yes, yippee, hoorah, huzzah, and halleluiah. Fist pumps are telling, as is a spontaneous happy dance. You can celebrate with yourself. "That's awesome! I love that!" You can also invite others to your celebration. Celebrating with others can feel awkward at first, it might not come naturally if you're not used to it. Putting it into practice can look like, "I'm feeling happy right now, can I share with you why?" It could be small. "I found a five-dollar bill in my old coat pocket." It could be worthy of a party, "I graduated; got promoted; finished chemo". You are allowed and encouraged to celebrate, and that kind of joy is contagious.

Sidebar: We might worry that others won't want to hear our good news, especially if their lives don't appear to be going so well. Do you resist sharing with others, fearing they will be envious? Do you feel guilty when things are going well for you? Warning bells might go off at the idea of celebrating. Things are going well?! That usually means something bad is going to happen. You might fear you'll jinx yourself if you notice it, speak about it or celebrate it. It might seem better to just fly under the radar. My experience, though, is that the more I celebrate, the more there is to celebrate.

Ap-pre-ci-a-tion: recognition and enjoyment of the good qualities of someone or something.

Recognition equals awareness. Enjoyment equals action. I think of appreciation as gratitude in action. Once again, we are noticing things going well and we want to acknowledge it in the moment. We're appreciating that it went well, or that we liked something that happened. Sharing that information, then, with another person is a great and important (in my opinion) practice. Those good feelings grow when we let them out of ourselves. When I recognize and celebrate the impact that an event had on me, I can share that appreciation with whoever had a part in it by simply stating, "When you _____ (share the action they took) I felt _____ (share an emotion) because _____ (share what you needed or wanted)". Sharing your appreciation gives the other person more information about how they actually impacted you, letting them know which behaviors of theirs helped make your life more wonderful. Letting people know when they contribute to our joy feeds us both. I think a full appreciation is richer than simply saying "thank you" but "thank you" might feel safer, and less awkward, and it is absolutely a worthwhile and valid primer tool.

In-spi-ra-tion: 1. The process of being mentally stimulated to do or feel something, especially to do something creative. 2. The drawing in of breath; inhalation.

Inspiration brings us to life via inhalation and it also brings life to us. It lifts us up. It makes us feel like we want to take action, like we want to create something. It gives us the ability and a reason to live a little bit longer. I feel like inspiration is an idea critical to a full life, but I believe that it is not given enough importance in our world today.

What inspires you? What lifts you up? You have probably felt inspired more than once in your life and you may already know something about what inspires you, but this is another area where there is so much more you can learn about your Authentic Self. It is also an area where we can infuse more life into our current reality.

Maybe you can recognize inspiring content when you see/hear/read it. You think, "Yes! I love that!" Maybe there are personalities out there whom you follow on social media because what they bring to the world feels inspiring, and what they offer uplifts you. This is a great way to experience inspiration - noticing the things created by others with which you resonate and noticing feeling more positive or hopeful when you are exposed to them. I can't say enough about how valuable this is, especially before and until we are able to connect with the specific ideas within ourselves that inspire us.

Side note: If you are not feeling uplifted by those you follow, or if you find yourself feeling cranky, discouraged, or depressed after exposure to their content, those folks are likely not in resonance with your Authentic Self. Even if millions of followers say differently, continuing to follow them may not be in your highest good.

It is so important to recognize what it feels like in your being when you are inspired. Do you smile, tear up, or get a lot more energized? Do you feel inclined to join the inspirer or take action of your own? Do you feel more relaxed knowing that there are people in the world who have a positive message? The next question you can ask yourself is, "Why?". What about that message, that vision, or that scene inspires you? That answer is significant. Just like with resonance or with envy, you are getting an insight into what you love, value, and aspire to see more of, but with that specific inspiration you are grabbing hold of that resonance and bringing more meaning directly into your life. You are weaving it through the fabric of your life and consequently making it stronger and more colorful.

Seek out inspiring content out there in the world and be sure to also tune into your own unique inner inspiration, as well. Which areas of life pique your interest? Where do you want to effect change? Do you dream of making the world a better place in some way? I don't know what that might look like for you but finding and bringing forth your own particular inspiration can make life richer and can make you want to move energy and take action. These are the things that can make you interested in showing up for another day in the world. These are the things inside of us that have the power to kick hopelessness and depression to the curb.

Once you discover your own vision, you can then move from there, from your essence and truth, no matter how tiny or large. Your own personal inspiration is one of the treasures living inside of you and it has the power to enrich you and your world. Whatever inspires you will definitely inspire others. I love watching Gabor Maté or other brilliant folks on social media, but more often than not I need to put into my own words the love and passion I have for life and the world. That is what I regularly feel inspired to do and it is what never fails to uplift me and my spirits.

Right Timing

When I am ready to make things happen in my life, when I have decided what I want and am taking steps in that direction, the idea that things happen when they are meant to happen, when we are ready and when it is the best time for them to happen, can take some getting used to. I can be pretty sure that I, with my big brain, know when things should happen and that usually just means when I want them to happen. When we are taking action on this path of authenticity, it can be scary, frustrating and confusing when things don't unfold in the way we expect. It can shake our faith in our vision or our plan. I frequently need to remind myself that the higher-ups have access to a bigger picture than I do and that things and their timing don't need to make sense to me.

Fortunately, I have had many experiences that have convinced me that the beings *up there* know far better than I do the best path and the best timing forward. If things aren't yet flowing, I can try to sit back, relax, and *let go and let god*.

Authenticity Applied – Motherhood

I have always known that I wanted to be a mother. Before my husband and I felt sure we were both ready for that journey, I had a miscarriage. I didn't even know I was pregnant, and it shook me. That miscarriage had me more than a little nervous when we officially started to try to become parents. I was optimistic though and was thrilled when I found out I was pregnant for the second time. The added bonus was that my sister, with whom I was closest, was also pregnant (we had both dreamed of being pregnant at the same time). Unfortunately, at my first doctor's visit I learned that I wasn't carrying a viable pregnancy. Needless to say, I was heartbroken, but I focused on counting the days/months until it was safe to try again.

"Surely the third time is the charm", I hoped when I again held a positive pregnancy test in my little hands. Sadly, at our first ultrasound visit we were given the devastating news that there was no heartbeat. After our gut-wrenching period of grief, my husband and I decided to set aside this painful path and move overseas where my husband had the opportunity to work for six months. It was an amazing, expanding, confidence-building experience to have. When we returned stateside, we decided we had the courage to try one more time.

We got pregnant easily (thankfully) once again and had access to a few medical interventions to help the pregnancy along. They actually worked and we made it out of the first trimester and through the second. I loved being pregnant and spent my days walking on air. At 27 weeks, though, my amniotic sac developed a tiny leak and I had to be placed on bed rest in the hospital until the baby was born. We made it almost two weeks more before that little being made her grand and dramatic entrance into the world.

From the first second I laid my eyes on our daughter, I knew why I was put on the earth. My heart had never held so much love and awe and wonder and my soul finally felt satisfied. All of the pain we endured before then was made worth it by that bright and tiny being.

I honestly believe that those miscarriages, while incredibly painful, kept me occupied until the time was actually best for us to be parents. I was much more ready for motherhood when she arrived than I was almost three years earlier. I also believe that if I had simply not gotten pregnant when I was trying, I would have been even more devastated and probably more determined to try to force the process. It felt like a bigger and better plan was in the works for me and my family.

We Are Creators

We humans are innately creative beings, though many of us might have bought into the story that the only people who are actually creative are those who are established *artists*. Only people who are professional painters, sculptors, musicians or authors, can call themselves creative. The rest of us probably don't have a creative bone in our bodies and don't deserve to call ourselves artists or creative beings. Well, those were the messages that I took in when I was growing up. The truth is that we are all creative and it is a part of our DNA. Creativity can take many different forms but when we are not spending some time creating and/or expressing ourselves in some way we can lose our connection to purpose and to meaning in our lives and that can, again, make getting out of bed in the morning a challenge. However, when we are able to, without the restricting fear of judgment, create and express freely, we are living our divine nature, our divine purpose, and it's hard to beat. When we are creating, we are plugged in, linked to the divine pipeline. Creativity allows your life force to flow through you, enlivening your being and the beings of others. It can be as simple as mindlessly doodling on paper, or as complex as imagining ways to tackle climate change. We all have gifts to bring to the world. Our creativity and expression are as vital to our own well-being as they are for the world. There are so many more ways to creatively contribute to the collective than we have been led to believe and the potential impact of that is staggeringly undervalued.

Authenticity Expressed

It's wonderful to learn about yourself and track what brings you to life. It's fantastic to call into your life more of that, but where this can really get good, where things can really elevate, is when you bring out your gifts and talents, when you actually offer them and express them in the world. To other people. Your actual authentic expression truly is my selfish aim here.

That might sound frightening, I realize, but it can instead be as my voice instructor says of performing, "This is my drug." When we share our gifts with another, we are gifted and uplifted just as much as the recipients are and maybe more.

Just like with all of these ideas I am bringing, it is a practice. You get to start where you are and go from there. You get to take your time and feel into your readiness.

Learning to have faith in the worth of your gifts and talents isn't always easy. There are so many potential messages floating around regarding who is worthy of bringing their talents forth, or of what is an actual legitimate *gift*. For some it can be confusing and nerve-wracking to even consider sharing our gifts with another person and depending on how much or little support one received growing up, the relationship with one's talents and gifts can be an estranged one.

I learned many silly ideas, during my life, about gifts and talents:
- If you didn't have it naturally, if you didn't show an inclination for it at a young age, don't bother pursuing it.

- If you can't make money from it, it's not worthwhile.
- Only people who are the best at a skill or talent are worthy of practicing or performing it.
- No one wants your flawed expression.
- Only serious gifts or talents should be pursued.
- You have to work really, really hard if you want to be good at something (talk about sucking the fun out of it).
- One's gifts and talents aren't really worth pursuing; the only legitimate, valid contribution to the world is your job. Everything else is frivolous.
- The only way I felt allowed to pursue my gifts and talents was if someone outside of myself validated my talent and encouraged me to pursue it. In other words, my own instincts, desires, and inclinations around this pursuit were not credible.

You might have guessed by now that I am a huge proponent of this exploration. I don't think this topic gets nearly enough attention in the world, nor do I think we get nearly enough support for finding and expressing our gifts and talents (unless we are an obvious prodigy). I'd love to see this pursuit valued more by our society, especially in schools. Because I have experienced so much joy in discovering and expressing mine, I want to know about and get to experience yours as well. I believe that a large source of depression in our world today is simply this missing piece in people's lives - the joy, satisfaction, and confidence associated with experiencing and expressing one's gifts, and having those gifts lovingly received by others. Aside from simply knowing that your very existence is a gift to the world, this is one of the most wonderful experiences possible.

Gifts and talents aren't only reserved for the "Arts", of course; people can be talented leaders, homemakers, athletes, problem solvers, and caregivers. People can have gifts that foster order, that contribute humor, imagination, inspiration and faith. Gifts and talents don't have to be big things, either; I am quite adept at, and thoroughly enjoy, untangling knots. Give me a tangled necklace or ball of knotted yarn and I am in ecstasy. I'm probably not going to make any money from it, but it is a fun and satisfying thing to do and worth recognizing the way it makes me feel. It makes me good at following a thread and it also benefits those with tangled necklaces or strings. I also love to sort things; I can be your own personal Coin Star if you'll let me. These feelings of joy, satisfaction, and confidence in ourselves, are only part of the payoff as we can't possibly know all of the ways in which our gifts and talents impact, uplift and enrich others.

If you are under the illusion that you have no gifts or talents, let me reassure you that you do, they are just likely buried. They probably weren't seen, valued, or accepted and that is why the exploration process moving forward must be treated with care. I have a particular passion for creating safety around the exploration and expression of one's gifts and talents because I view them as so very valuable and sacred and I know how easily they can be snuffed out. I view the unexpressed parts of ourselves as precious and that is why I encourage you to be very discerning with whom and where you choose to share your gifts and talents, or what you wish them to be (remember envy?).

If you have known gifts and talents that you are already sharing with the world, I would still encourage you to practice inquiry and exploration of your relationship to these gifts or undiscovered ones. As I have said several times, there is much more to us than we likely know so why not take yourself on a treasure hunt? Once you have found your treasure, you can practice bringing it into the light for others to enjoy.

Remember, locating and acknowledging your gifts is only the start. Practicing sharing them (safely) and then paying attention to what that experience is like for you, are the crucial next steps (for you and for us). Are the old fears coming up? Are you having more fun than you imagined you would? Was someone moved or touched by what you shared? What was that like?

If I could accompany each and every one of you on this journey I would. As I have said, talents can be seemingly small and insignificant, radically profound and world changing, or somewhere in between. They are all worthwhile, no matter the size. It is my hope that the world (and therefore I) will get to experience your brilliance, whatever that looks like and however much of it you are ready to share.

Side note: We must absolutely include your emotional expression in all of this talk of authentic expression, whether that be love, anger, frustration, or sadness. As humans we need opportunities, and safe spaces, for this kind of vulnerable expression. Though we may have been taught to believe that they are unwelcome, our emotions are gifts too, especially our love. Part of the pain and grief of the loss of a loved one is the loss of that outlet for our loving expression. May Sarton says that "The gift turned inward, unable to be given, becomes a heavy burden, even sometimes a kind of poison. It is as though the flow of life were backed up." I have experienced this discomfort for myself and it is part of the reason why I am writing this book.

Finding the Vision/Touching the Dream

Finding and sharing your gifts and talents can be such a fulfilling experience, and this is indeed exactly what I am promoting here, and yet, there may be even more to discover than that. Maybe there is a specific vision, a hidden soul dream inside of you that only you can realize. Do you sometimes feel this niggling little sense that your being has something specific to express, create, or manifest? Do you feel like you have a destiny to fulfill? Maybe you have learned that you love to noodle around on the piano, and that is wonderful, fulfilling and joy producing, but maybe your *true* soul dream is to perform your own compositions. Or perhaps, like me, you love to play around with writing, but you really secretly dream of telling your story and having others read it/hear it. Maybe you're a cook by day but at night you dream of feeding the world. Do you have an idea that keeps coming into your head, and it has done so for years? Is there something inside that if it were to manifest it would feel too good to be true? Author Julia Cameron calls this *The Vein of Gold* in her book of the same name, and I love that imagery. Is there a deep and shining tread of brilliance in you, waiting to be unearthed? Maybe you are at this point or maybe not, but I suspect there is some version of this vein of gold in everyone. If it isn't speaking to you now that is totally fine and valid, just pay attention and know that it might happen someday. Maybe it only happens at certain times in life, when the conditions are ripe. All I know is that in some (or all of us) there is a vision, a soul dream, that is begging to be heard and begging to be brought forth into the world, by the only person who can do it and it feels like the worldly manifestation of your true essence. Who knows? Maybe there is more than one. Maybe when you have brought forth one there is another waiting in the wings. But for me especially, right now, it feels like there is an end-of-the-road dream, the pinnacle - the thing that is the embodiment of my unique energetic signature. I love this book more than anything else I have written and listening to myself in order to write it has been my biggest act of self-love thus far. It feels like the magical culmination of all of that research, practice and experimentation.

Side note: Let's talk about humility for a second. In order to believe that we can share our gifts and visions with the world, that we are worthy, we need to have a certain amount of audacity or hubris on board. Many of us have been taught that being humble is the correct way to be. Who am I to dare to imagine that greatness lives in me? My own particular idea of humility included keeping my head down and staying invisible - blessed are the meek, and all of that. Well, that simply won't work when you have something that the world needs. At some point every performer, artist, leader, and visionary has to kick that false humility to the curb and find the courage and the belief in themselves to bring their gift to others.

The whole intention behind finding and sharing our gifts is to experience inspiration, joy, and fun within ourselves, and to give others those experiences as well. I find this to be an overlooked source of goodness and positivity in the world. To me it is a literal untapped goldmine of happiness.

Here are some tools and explorations to help you discover which talents are in there, how to recognize them, and how to bring them forth.

Exploring:
Stream of Consciousness Writing – instructions are in the Appendix
Creation writing – instructions are in the Appendix
If you could wave a magic wand what would you make happen?
What would you love to give to the world if you weren't worried about making money?
How are you currently being creative?
How have you been creative in the past?
What kinds of creations have you had an interest in or inkling of experiencing?
Is there a creative fantasy you have been harboring?
Did you have any unusual talents as a child?

Expression:
What do you want to be known for?
When was the last time you remember sharing your expression with another?
When and where can you practice more expression?
Dare to create something and share it with someone safe.
How did it feel to express it?
How did it feel to share it with another person?

Potential Forms of Creative Expression:
Writing – journaling, prose, poetry, storytelling, essays
Poetry reading
Performing/speaking
Storytelling
Music – voice or instrument, composition, production
Open mic opportunities
Sharing your story – at a 12-step meeting, a church, storytelling events
Crafting your personal aesthetic
Crafting the aesthetic of your space
Dancing – alone, in a class, socially
Sewing
Knitting
Flower arranging
Organizing
Working on electronics
Math
Engineering
Counseling
Politics
Building something
Restoring something
Working on cars
Making a social media video or channel

Writing a letter – to someone, to a politician, to the editor
Cooking/baking
Decorating
Woodworking

Service as Expression:
Volunteer for an organization connected to something meaningful
Donate time, money, and/or skills
Send letters to refugees, people in prison, people in the military
Make a care package for the homeless
Pray

Expressing Your Life Force by Moving Energy:
Dancing
Acting
Wiggling
Athletics
Tidying up your space
Deep cleaning your space or another's
Running errands
Walking

Expressing Relationally:
Play The Noticing Game
Play If You Really Knew Me
Tell someone how you are feeling or share the impact they have had
Share your appreciation with a person you know or a business
Write a fan letter to one of your important people

The Gift of a Peak Experience

Abraham Maslow coined the phrase "peak experience" to refer to "powerful, meaningful experiences in which individuals seem to transcend the self, be at one with the world, and feel completely self-fulfilled". He found that they can occur for individuals in their pursuit of self-actualization. This concept really resonated with me and I have loved having a term to apply to each of the amazing, magical and wonderful experiences that I have had in my life, mostly as a result of this path of authenticity. Which of your past experiences would you put into this category? It's helpful to remind yourself that you have indeed had some. If you truly can't come up with any, I feel confident they are on the horizon.

Authenticity Applied – The Christmas Pageant

In 1998, a musically talented high school friend contacted me because he had created a Christmas pageant for our local parish, and he needed a baby Jesus. He wanted to know if he could borrow my 3-month-old baby, Glenn. Aware of my love of singing, he also invited me to join the angel chorus. Naturally, I enthusiastically agreed. When the group first got together to hear the music he wanted to use, I fell in love with "Breath of Heaven" by Amy Grant. "I want to sing that song," I thought to myself, envious of the young woman who was set to play the role of Mary. I didn't think any more about it until a few days later when my friend told me that the young woman had developed laryngitis and he needed me to fill in as Mary. It turns out I wasn't the only one who wanted me to sing that song. I (despite my advanced age of 35) was able to play the role of Mother Mary, sing that beautiful song, and have my own child as Jesus. This was a peak experience indeed, and it was a tremendous gift to get to have a role in the pageant's existence. The love, grace, and holy vibes that emanated from this event were felt by everyone in the church and I was in heaven getting to use my voice for a higher purpose. Side note: Glenn, who had cried all through dress rehearsal, was a perfect angel, er baby Jesus, through the actual performance.

Acknowledge/Affirm/Accept

I have certainly mentioned quite often the importance of *awareness* on this whole journey of authenticity - we can't change what we can't see - but finding our way to actual acceptance of who we authentically are is our ultimate goal. It can be difficult to impossible to share or bring forth aspects of yourself that you aren't able to accept.

I begin with the idea of simply taking stock of where one's life is in the current reality. Ask yourself what is *real* now? With awareness and acknowledgment of what is real you get to get curious about how you really feel about that reality. What emotions get brought up in you when you face those facts? How do you feel about the fact that you are in debt, or don't have the physical health you would like to have?

Side note: I advise setting up some support for yourself as you work through this process. Start small, take your time, make a comfortable and safe environment and, if it feels appropriate, share any of your discoveries with someone safe.

The next step is to understand how you got to this reality. What valid circumstances led to this? It can be so helpful and freeing to see this, to understand that there may have been things beyond your control or that you were simply doing the best you could with what you knew at the time. We tend to be needlessly hard on ourselves and seeing what led us to where we are can help us soften on ourselves and be more realistic and accepting of that reality.

Next we get to forgive and accept ourselves for ending up where we are, in any area of our life. We all deserve this.

What is the current situation?
In your social life
In your financial life
In your work life
In your mind
In your body
In your spirit

How do you feel about it?
Why? What do you need/want?
How did you get there?

Tell yourself that you did the best you could or that you forgive yourself for _____. (For living beyond your means, for example.)

Try saying, "Even though _____ (insert reality/situation here. For example: 'Even though I have accrued a lot of debt,') I love and accept myself unconditionally". Even if that sentence feels untrue, because you aren't so forgiving of yourself yet, simply intending to love and accept yourself unconditionally, for whatever is real, will help your being relax and come out of the shadows a little bit more. And it will help your being get in alignment with that intention.

If You Can Dream It

Living in alignment requires less energy than living out of alignment. Living in alignment has a profound positive impact on the whole of our beings, on our physiology, and on our psychology. We have more energy and less stress with all of the implications of that. Living in alignment can't help but impact every single aspect of our lives and everyone in them. Just imagine what's possible when we don't have to devote so much energy to contorting ourselves in order to fit into our lives as they are, or in order to not disturb anyone else's.

What could it feel like to get relief from suppressing our desires and dreams? Our nervous systems relax when we are in our truth. We have gifts and talents to bring to the world. Getting to spend our time and energy doing the things we love and were born to do, (no matter how much or little time it is) is in itself a gift. Getting to share our gifts with the world is an even greater payoff. We have everything we need in order to accomplish all of this and we will have a positive impact materially, practically and energetically on the world.

do not choose the lesser life. do you hear me. do you hear me. choose the life that is. yours. the life that is seducing your lungs. that is dripping down your chin.

- Nayyirah Waheed

SECTION V: Doing the Math

What lives within us is more powerful than any weapon ever created. It is my belief that the potential that exists in the world, if more people lived authentically and saw the truth about who we all are, is mind blowing and revolutionary. As I said in the beginning of this book, we are living in a time fraught with anxiety, gloom and doom. Social media's role in stirring up such dread is, by now, well documented. To believe that we as a culture, as a global collective, are limited in the same ways we are taught to see ourselves individually, could only logically lead to hopelessness. But, if there is more to people individually, as I certainly believe there is, then there is definitely more to people collectively and from there our imaginations can take off.

We as humans have had the inspiration, genius and audacity to undertake incredible feats of art, invention and engineering (heart transplants, space stations, architectural wonders). Look at the audacious creations which come out of Hollywood alone. People keep raising the bar on what is possible physically, athletically, technologically; we can't possibly be at the limits, yet, of what is possible.

Imagine the additional potential creativity available when more people aren't using their energy and resources for lower vibratory pursuits but rather are inspired to bring higher ideas forward into the world. I am talking about actually creating world peace, sustainable renewable energy, more medical miracles, an end to global hunger, not to mention more of the breathtaking beauty we are capable of creating. I am imagining a world where harmony, unity and collaboration eclipse greed, competition and separation; where we can trust that it makes more fiscal sense to be inclusive, equitable, just, and environmentally responsible; where we hold the value of the arts in as much esteem as the sciences and where the line between the two is actually blurred.

There is so much more available to us individually, and therefore collectively, when we are aligned with our Authentic Selves. When we are aligned with our Authentic Selves, we are plugged into the truth about who we are. When we are plugged into the truth about who we are, we are plugged into the genius of the universal mind and truly anything is possible.

We Are All Connected

There are many incredible stories about people experiencing a larger reality; stories of people hearing loved ones from across great distance; stories of people spontaneously healing from life threatening illness; medical science unable to explain what caused the heart to heal or someone's tumors to disappear. What if the same thing were possible but on a global scale. What if it was already happening? I believe that the intentions of many have been influencing collective outcomes for eons. Why not dare to imagine such possibilities? Why not imagine and envision the healing of our planet and the beings who inhabit it? Why not help that dream along? I regularly take time to send love and light to people who are working on solutions to the world's problems.

I believe that there is an unlimited supply of energy available to us at all times; in the form of love, in the form of wisdom, inspiration, genius, kindness, and action. All of it. We have learned a different story, so again, we are not having that experience. And once again, not knowing this doesn't stop it from being true and the only question is what is getting in the way of living in that reality? What ideas or beliefs have we taken in personally and collectively that have us imagining a scary and limiting future; a future with restricted possibilities? If we have access to everything: energy, knowledge, and support, then we can create the future of our dreams, both individually and collectively. We have everything we need to get everything we desire and the more of us who hold that vision as truth, the better for us all. This is what inspires me; this certainty that together we can up-level, uplift all of humanity and have more and more of what we desire – what I believe our souls came here to experience.

Back to Dr. Hawkins's work on the levels of emotional vibration, he discovered that any being vibrating at a level below 200 is inherently in a destructive mindset, but once a person is vibrating at 200 (courage) or above, they have entered into a productive, life-giving consciousness. The collective implication of this is massive. Dr. Hawkins asserts that the impact of one person vibrating at a level of 600 (peace), for example, can counterbalance ten million people vibrating at a level of 200. One person sitting alone in their room praying peace for humanity, or one person fully engaged in expressing their inspiring gift, can uplift the world. If one person can have that powerful of an impact, simply by becoming the best version of themselves, imagine what is possible when more people join their intentions. The result is logarithmically expanded with the potential for miracles.

There are More of Us

There are many notable organizations who recognize the power in our interconnectedness and who are endeavoring to bring the full potential of humanity into the manifest world. Here are two that I have become acquainted with.

The HeartMath Institute has been studying the impact of consciously coming into resonance with other people and has a division called the Global Coherence Initiative where they are "Expanding our capacity to love. The Global Coherence™ Initiative is a science-based, co-creative project to unite people in heart-focused love and intention, to facilitate the shift in global consciousness from instability and discord to compassionate care, cooperation and increasing peace." They offer an opportunity each month on the full moon, to connect with others who are intending to bring more love and care to the world. HeartMath's Global Coherence research "incorporates a wide variety of scientific data to gain new insight into the interconnectedness between humanity, plants, and animals and the Sun and Earth's magnetic energy." It's not just a sweet idea, they have the actual data to show that we are indeed connected to one another via our hearts and that we can use that connection for the greater good. So inspiring.

I learned about Auroville, an intentional village in India, while I was getting my yoga teacher certification and I have not stopped thinking about it since. They speak directly to my belief in the potential of the human collective. "Auroville wants to be a universal town where men and women of all countries are able to live in peace and progressive harmony above all creeds, all politics and all nationalities. The purpose of Auroville is to realize human unity." They bring together people committed to their highest expression and study the resulting synergy in their effort to uplift the world.

These are just two examples in a world full of people who are working to contribute more to the collective. Once you start to look for evidence that there is more positivity and more possibility out there you will begin to see it everywhere.

Manifesting the Genius

What could it look like to have more people living in alignment, sharing their genius with the world? What is possible when people feel brave enough to pursue their ideas, bring them to the world and have others recognize and support their genius? We are form and spirit and so much of how we live in the world and how the world approaches life here, discounts what that means. What would it look like to not just believe in a benevolent force *out there* but to also know that you carry that within, and that that force wants us all to operate from this expansive idea? I hope to inspire more of that. I believe that we have what we need to solve the world's problems, we just need to create a greater level of safety within and without in order to allow the genius to come through and be expressed.

A scientifically controlled study conducted by German researchers at the University of Kassel has shown that while the chest area of an average person emits only 20 photons of light per second, someone who meditates on their heart center and sends love and light to others emits an amazing 100,000 photons per second. That is 5,000 times more than the average human being. Numerous studies have also shown that when these photons are infused with a loving and healing intent, their frequency and vibration increase to the point where they can literally change matter, heal disease, and transform negative events.

Ten minutes of meditating on compassion, on kindness for others, and you will see its effects all day. That's the way to maintain a calm and joyous mind.

- From the Book of Joy: Lasting Happiness in a Changing World by Dalai Lama

There is a vitality, a life force, a quickening that is translated through you into action, and there is only one of you in all time, this expression is unique, and if you block it, it will never exist through any other medium, it will be lost. The world will not have it. It is not your business to determine how good it is, not how it compares with other expressions. It is your business to keep it yours clearly and directly, to keep the channel open. You do not even have to believe in yourself or your work. You have to keep open and aware directly to the urges that motivate you. Keep the channel open.

- Martha Graham

CONCLUSION

You matter. In fact, you are everything. There is only one you and your mandate is to unearth your magnificent essence. It is a path, a sometimes stressful and painful one. It is a process, a sometimes long and confusing one. But given the incredible potential wealth of gifts available, how can you refuse? Well, I know all too well how you can refuse. I know how you can hide, sabotage and distract but it is my hope that I have offered enough inspiration, faith in yourself and in the process to counteract your natural resistance. You have already been on this path, both consciously and unconsciously and now you get to step fully, with both feet, into the light in a brighter and more powerful way. Hooray for all of us.

Jody Pignolet

Authenticity Applied – Not for the Faint of Heart

It feels a little weird and edgy to share the following story, especially since I still don't know today exactly what it means, but I want to share it because it is so personally potent and meaningful and because many other people have experiences that don't quite fit into any box. This story, more importantly, is an example of the power of this path of authenticity, an example of the potential magic, anguish and ecstasy when one chooses to manifest their Authentic Self in the world. This is a story of synchronicity, resonance and divine orchestration and if I hadn't believed in those things, I might have missed them or I might have dismissed them, thinking I was not quite right in my head.

One summer, when my kids were fairly self-sufficient, I had been doing a lot of journaling (and praying) about finding my purpose, my work in the world. My husband was a successful businessman and the breadwinner, and I was feeling ready to expand beyond my role as mother and homemaker. I had a pretty good idea of my talents; the list was actually long, but I didn't know how to turn them fit into a valued or marketable vocation out in the world. I had a deep yearning (partly driven by my ego and old ideas of worth, and partly by my soul) to find my calling.

One evening during that summer, my kids and I watched a movie. I was so profoundly impacted by the movie that I had to watch it again by myself the next day to learn more about why that was. I had two responses to rewatching it, one was what I call "soul crying" – I wept from a very deep place, and I couldn't explain why. The story was indeed touching but my tears didn't seem to be about that. The second response I had was a thought: "I'd love to be a part of creating something that beautiful".

The film was wonderfully uplifting, and the music was just as inspiring so the following day I went to the store to buy the DVD and the CD. The clerk told me that the man who wrote the film lived in our town. "I would love to meet the person who wrote such a beautiful story," I replied. My message was apparently received by the universe because a few weeks later I learned that this man was going to be answering questions at our local theater following the screening of the film. (It turns out he didn't actually live in my town.) Naturally, I went to the screening. When the writer walked on stage after the movie, I was instantly and categorically attracted to him. "You're a married woman," I admonished myself, but when he announced that he was doing a screenwriting workshop the next day I also said, "I'm totally going to that." "You are?" a surprised part of me questioned. I went to that workshop and two things happened there: 1. I listened with rapt attention and absorbed everything that man said. 2. I learned that screenwriting was actually a great fit for me creatively, and I was inspired and very interested in learning more. I had fantasized for years about writing a book but bringing it to life via this form made much more sense to me and my visual orientation. Not to mention, here was a mentor, one in whom I was very interested, offering his help.

I took off writing almost immediately with my limited skillset and eventually reached out to the writer for help. The vibes, despite the fact that we were only communicating via email, were electric from the start.

Jody Pignolet

I tried to downplay them because, well, having electric vibes with another man is usually frowned upon when one is in a committed monogamous relationship as I was. I dove into my screenplay (ironically, one about a woman meeting a man and remembering a profound past life experience featuring him). I actually completed the screenplay; it had a beginning, a middle and an end. I had never accomplished such a feat and if I did nothing else with it, I was very proud of myself. I gave it to the writer to read, keeping the synchronistic details to myself, until he actually told me that my story and the timing of my reaching out were very synchronistic for him. Oh boy, this seemed to have a life beyond my own little ego machinations. He then told me that he was coming to my town again for a week-long screenwriting workshop. Great news, except for one little detail: I was married, and the rest of my being was counting the days until we met for real, in person.

After he told me he was coming to town I literally curled up in the fetal position on my couch and cried. What was happening? Why the strong reactions, I wondered? I called my sister for counsel. I did not want to have yearnings for another man and the prospect of feeling a potentially addictive pull shook me. I had to go to the workshop, though, it was too synchronistic of a connection to run from it in fear. I had been given another fantastic idea for a film, and my feelings for this man aside, I loved writing screenplays. This was an answer to my prayers, and I could see myself pursuing this professionally.

My husband and I had had a very transparent marriage for many years, so I shared with him what was happening. You can imagine that it didn't go over well, but God bless him, he stayed open and supported my moving forward. I met with the writer when he arrived in town and we talked and talked. It felt like we were related somehow or came from the same planet. I told my husband that I needed to see what this resonance was about, that's how strongly I felt about it. I wasn't assuming it was meant to be a romantic connection. I was open to collaboration, or more mentorship or perhaps we were soul family and my family and his could be great friends. I was open to all of these ideas because this sort of resonance didn't feel like it needed to be restricted to romance and I had learned that *attraction* took many forms. I had also evolved to the point where my yearning for that kind of attention had lessened considerably over the years. The tricky thing was that one doesn't just bring up these kinds of thoughts with a virtual stranger. If we didn't have some sort of actual karmic/soul connection, then the only other explanation was that I must be out of my mind. I had certainly had my share of nutty moments over the years but when I did the math and added up all of the synchronicity, I had to conclude that this was a karmic/soul connection. Fortunately, so did my husband.

My conscious self had forgotten until much later after meeting him that before I met him in real life, I had a very vivid dream. I dreamed that I was with some benevolent beings who were taking me to meet a man, someone who was very important to my soul, but they made sure I knew that it wasn't the time for us to be together in each other's lives, just that we were going to meet up in this world. We walked into a classroom. He was a teacher working with young adults. We saw each other and hugged. I will never forget that feeling of being home. And then, in the dream, we simply parted company. I will forever love those beings who helped me prepare for our real-life meeting.

We are no longer in each other's lives; I think it just got weird and apparently it wasn't meant to be. The resulting gifts, however, were monumental, which is why I am so glad I forged ahead with a connection that on paper seemed fraught with risk. Because of that connection, I found my passion, my confidence, and my voice as a writer and a storyteller; I dared to believe that I really had a lot more to say and to offer the world. I learned that despite being drawn to this man and the sadness of not having him in my life, finding and expressing my own voice was a greater joy than any need I had for him, for looking outside of myself. I may have wanted him in my life, but I discovered that I wanted my whole self more. My husband and I, too, just kept showing up, telling the truth, and tending to our emotional needs, which allowed us to move through this massive opportunity for growth and come out closer on the other side.

Authenticity Applied – What It All Comes Down To

I have talked about the fact that most of my adult life has been focused on this path of self-discovery and spirituality and I have long believed it was preparing me for more in my life, a bigger role, a louder voice perhaps. That all may still be true, but the real proving ground – the arena in which I got to put into practice most everything I had learned and experienced so far – was the experience of walking with my youngest adult child, Glenn, through their dire mental health struggles and addiction to heroin.

If any of you have dealt with the struggles of addiction and/or mental illness, or have loved someone who struggles, you know how confusing, stressful, terrifying, devastating and heartbreaking that road can be. The story of our family's trip down that road reflects my take on why the principles in this book are so important and why they are so valuable for more than just oneself.

Our youngest child, Glenn, had had a lifetime of difficulty being in a human body. They (remember, Glenn's pronouns are they/them) are a bright, shiny, talented, and sensitive being and life had been a largely challenging endeavor for them. So, when their bumpy road ultimately led to heroin use and addiction, it wasn't a huge surprise. It was, however, a huge nightmare for all of us, and by far the most challenging thing I had ever gone through.

If I hadn't had a well-established relationship with a power greater than myself, if I hadn't known that we weren't alone in navigating this, the weight of this experience surely would have crushed me. If I hadn't learned to trust the guidance of my spiritual support squad and my own intuition (my husband's and Glenn's too), and if I hadn't had the courage to follow it, I would have lost my mind in the cacophony of ideas, advice, opinions, and options swirling around us during those years. If I hadn't had experience with creative and outside-of-the-box thinking, we might have just blindly followed the path that addicts, and their loved ones, are encouraged to take; a path that ended up not being the right one for our kid or for us.

If my husband and I hadn't already established some connecting and partnering skills, this would have absolutely torn us apart. If I didn't already know who Glenn was at their core and if I wasn't able to reflect that truth back to them as often as I possibly could, they might have continued to believe that they were a loser with nothing to offer the world, and kept on behaving as if that were true. If I hadn't known that Glenn came into the world with things to learn, I would have blamed myself completely for what they were going through.

If I hadn't learned how to anchor myself and my mind into the present moment, I would have terrorized myself far more than I actually did with thoughts of *what ifs* and *what could bes*. The present moment, where all is well, also gave me a place to return to and enjoy a respite from the stress of this journey.

If I hadn't learned through all of my experiences that I do have the power to co-create with the divine, that I can dare to dream up and fully imagine the reality I wish to see, we might have settled for less than what we believed was possible and what we have now which is an amazing, loving, funny, and gifted human who is completely free from the grips of heroin. Finally, if Glenn were not still here to tell their story then the world would miss out on all of the awesomeness that they have brought and continue to bring, most especially in the form of their precious daughter.

Coming Full Circle

You came into this world as a beautiful and bright being full of your brand of brilliance and potential. Your spirit-self came into your physical existence with a to-do list of lessons to learn and potential to fulfill. The limiting and negative ideas you learned about yourself, about others and about the world have been getting in the way of you being your best self and of living your best life. Life may have dulled your shine, but that shine never really went away. Everything authentic and original about you is still there, it still exists and wants to be discovered. Your being wants this, your being needs this, and your being deserves this. The world wants, needs and deserves it too. The world wants what only you can bring: your Authentic Self.

I believe that the world wants more and more people living in alignment and vibrating at higher frequencies. That is the fuel that can move the world in the direction so many of us are dreaming of. This is absolutely the story I am dreaming of and this is the story I am writing. And then we all get to shine.

Our deepest fear is not that we are inadequate.
Our deepest fear is that we are powerful beyond measure.
It is our light, not our darkness that most frightens us.
We ask ourselves, "Who am I to be brilliant, gorgeous, talented, fabulous?"
Actually, who are you not to be? You are a child of God.
Your playing small does not serve the world.
There is nothing enlightened about shrinking so that other people won't feel insecure around you.
We are all meant to shine, as children do.
We were born to manifest the glory of God that is within us.
It's not just in some of us; it's in everyone.
And as we let our own light shine, we unconsciously give other people permission to do the same.
As we are liberated from our own fear, our presence automatically liberates others.
- Marianne Williamson

And Then We All Get to Shine

APPENDIX

Critical Elements

Below is a list of the elements, skills and actions that I have found to be helpful, if not critical, in the pursuit of a full and authentic life. Beyond that you will find instructions for some of the practices that have changed my world.

Pausing and anchoring into the present moment.
Having agency over your breath.
Creating safety within and without.
Having a belief in something (anything) bigger than your individual self.
Having experiences of noticing and feeling your authentic awesomeness and anchoring those experiences into your being.
Finding and releasing limiting ideas from the past.
Noticing and celebrating the good stuff.
Noticing/feeling/recognizing inspiration within and without.
Touching your dreams, visions and desires.
Creating time and space to dream.
Moving energy - physically, mentally, emotionally, and spiritually.
Finding balance - physical, mental, emotional and spiritual.
Connecting with nature and the elements.
Spending time in fun, play, and laughter.
Spending time in meaningful activity - whether that be what you do to earn money or not.
Spending time in creativity.
Spending time in human connection.

Essentially, we are:

> Grabbing insight from the past
>
> Tending to and enlivening the present
>
> Setting the course for our dreams and visions of the future

Finding Presence

Gaining the ability to connect to the body and to the present moment might be one of the most important and useful tools for cultivating authenticity. Every moment begins anew when you are connected to the now, so beginning your day with a moment of presencing, or anchoring into the present moment before an important talk or event, gives you a solid base to move from. Having that relationship and awareness with your body and the present moment gives you a touchpoint to return to when you get triggered or lose your center throughout the day. It also allows you to redirect your mind and prevent it from creating all kinds of stories when you are dysregulated.

Connecting with the present moment:

Connecting to your breath is the quickest, most reliable way of connecting with the present moment. Simply bringing your awareness to your body as it breathes itself will anchor you in the now. By simply and easily following your inhalations and the exhalations for as long as you would like or for as long as you are able, you can step away from tension, drama or fear. You may count the individual breaths, or you may count through the length of the inhalation and count through the length of the exhalation. Traditional practices agree that practicing a five second inhalation and a five second exhalation is optimal for regulating the nervous system. Simply bring your awareness back to your breath when your attention goes elsewhere. Your breath is available to you in every moment, meaning you are never without this tool.

Tuning into your physical senses is another foolproof strategy for connecting to the present moment. When you are attuned to what you are feeling through touch, sound, sight, smell, or taste, you can't be anyplace else but the present.

*You can record yourself reading the following meditations or have someone read them to you while you practice.

Find yourself in a comfortable position, either seated or lying down. Feel your body in contact with whatever surface is supporting it. Eyes can be open or closed, whichever is most comfortable for you. Bring your attention to the information coming in through your skin. Do you feel warmth or coolness? Is there air moving over your skin? Maybe you feel the fabric of your clothes or the compression of your shoes. There is no right or wrong answer, you are only experiencing your world, this moment, through touch. Whenever your attention drifts simply bring it back to your senses.

Next, bring your attention to your ears, bringing awareness to the sounds coming in through your ears. They might be close or far away, see how many different sounds you can detect or try to tune into one sound more finely, do you notice any new details?

Next, bring your attention to your nose, feel the air moving in and out of your nostrils. Do you notice any odors capturing your attention? Maybe your lotion or soap, or your neighbor's cooking? Maybe nothing comes at first but the longer you sit with it the more easily you can smell something subtle.

Bring your awareness to your mouth. Can you find any tastes there? Move your tongue around in your mouth, do you notice anything subtle, anything new?

Lastly, if your eyes have been closed, open them. Slowly let the light enter your eyes, allow the information to enter your eyes as opposed to looking out towards something specific. Slowly allow your eyes to drift over the space, allowing curiosity to lead. Are you seeing anything that you haven't noticed before?

After a few minutes of this sensory attention, bring your awareness back to your body. What do you notice? How are you feeling? Take a few minutes to become aware of your whole being before moving on with your day.

Head-to-toe awareness:

Again, find yourself in a comfortable position. Bring your awareness (you could experience this as something you see, sense, or feel) to the top of your head, allow your attention to drift over your forehead, softening any tension as you move along. Continue to move your awareness gently along your face, see where there might be tension you can release. Bring the attention down your neck to your shoulders, soften here. Take both arms at once, or one at a time, releasing tension as you go, all the way to your fingertips. Return to your shoulders and travel with your awareness down your chest, back and belly. Soften any tension, find ease in your breath. Move over your pelvic region, releasing and softening. Bring your awareness to the thighs, knees, lower legs and feet. Bring your awareness over your toes and to the soles of your feet. Spend some time here, feeling into the quality of sensation on the soles. Try to soften tension and imagine your inhalation traveling all the way down to your soles, bringing life and energy there. Now imagine that your breath is traveling all the way up your legs, up your torso, up your arms, up your neck, over your face and ending at the top of your head. Linger there for a few breath cycles. Tune into your experience of your body now. What do you notice? Take a few more minutes with yourself before you get up and move back into your day.

Grounding Meditation:

Grounding is a word that can mean simply connecting to your body and therefore becoming grounded in the moment, or it can also mean generating a deeper connection with the earth below you. Find yourself in a comfortable seated position. Eyes open or closed, whichever feels best to you. Bring your awareness (by seeing, sensing or feeling) to your feet in contact with the floor or your shoes. What does that feel like, what do you notice? Next bring your awareness to the feeling of your bottom in contact with your seat or chair. What do you notice there? From the center of your pelvic floor, imagine a root or a cord traveling down to the floor, through the floor and into the earth. Imagine it traveling through the layers of the earth as far as you would like to go, all the way to the core if that feels right. Imagine that you can feel the welcoming quality of the earth's energy, reassured that you belong there. Spend as much time there as you like or have time for. Whenever you are ready you can bring that cord back up through the earth, through the floor and back up through your pelvic floor. You can anchor it in the center of your pelvis, or you can bring it up further through your torso to your heart or you can take it through the top of your head and out into the cosmos. You can simply experience the expansiveness out there or find a celestial body that calls to you. Receive that expansion and openness from wherever you traveled and when you feel ready, bring it back along the cord to your body. You may connect it to your heart or allow that energy to fill your whole being. Allow the energies to mingle with your cells for a few moments before you move on from the exercise and into your day.

Walking meditation:

Bringing oneself into a meditative state need not only happen in a cross-legged seated position. It is possible to use the rhythm of walking to induce meditation. It is helpful to find a place to walk where you will have few distractions (though it is not essential) and where you don't need to put a lot of focus on remaining safe (from quickly moving cars or bikes, for instance). Set a timer or walk until you feel ready to stop. You may simply begin by finding your connection with your body, by feeling the soles of your feet or by tuning into your body breathing itself.

Once you feel that level of presence you may take your first step, slowly, mindfully, and then the next. You might want to inhale with one foot forward, exhale with the next, or step right and left on the inhale, right and left on the exhale. A mantra is a word or phrase that you repeat either aloud or in your mind, and it is helpful in keeping your focus in the present. The Sanskrit mantra So Ham, for example, is very powerful as it essentially means, "I am that". Repeat "So" as you breathe in and "ham" as you breathe out. If your attention drifts, simply bring it back to your breath, mantra or steps. When your time is up, take a few minutes to look around and connect yourself visually with your surroundings. Once you have had this experience you can call on it anytime and practice mindfulness as you are moving through your day.

Moving energy:

Stuck energy, life force that isn't flowing as it should is a natural part of life. While that may be true it doesn't mean that we should just leave it where it is. Stuck energy can result in relationship tension or stagnancy, physical tension, lethargy, maladies, mental tension or stagnancy, and spiritual depression. Fortunately, there are so many ways that we can move that energy, emphasis on *move*, inside our bodies and within our environment. When my husband and I are in a tense conversation sometimes I just need to get up and clean while we talk. Going for a walk around the neighborhood is a great way to loosen up the body and the mind. Journaling is a fantastic way to get clarity by moving one's thoughts out of one's head. There are wonderful breathing exercises for moving stagnant energy, focusing the attention on where in the body the energy is stuck. Exercise, laughter, singing loudly, yelling into a pillow or out in nature, crying, dancing, wiggling, massage or other body work. Anything that gets the life force flowing, will help clear out stuck energy. Refer back, also, to the list in Intentionally Raising Your Vibration for more ideas.

Finding What's Inside

Below are a few tools for discovering, on a deeper level, what lives inside of you and where you would like to go on your journey.

Heart Space Meditation:

The Heart Space Meditation is one of my favorite tools. It shows me so much about what is going on in my inner world and it helps my continued connection to the vibration of love. It also helps me with difficulties in my relationships.

Begin with the above Grounding Meditation. When you find yourself feeling calm and connected to your being bring your attention to your heart. Feel the aliveness present in this area of your body. Imagine you are entering this space, either through a door or whatever opening organically presents itself. You are entering your Heart Space. Perhaps you find yourself on a path or in an open space. You might be in a room or in nature, there is no right or wrong thing to imagine. You might not be aware of anything at all visually but instead you feel it or sense it, there are many ways to experience guided meditation. Try to get a sense of what this space looks or feels like. Again, there is no right answer here. It is simply your heart space communicating with you. Find a way to be comfortable there. If it is a place you can see, imagine a sweet place to sit, if you aren't visual, imagine feeling calm and relaxed there. Now, you may simply stay here for a little while and see what happens or you may ask for information. You may ask for a conversation with someone special by asking for someone specific or by asking for any unresolved connection to be resolved. See/feel/sense who comes forward. I have had many, many healing conversations with loved ones (and not so loved ones) in my heart space. It is a safe place to say whatever you need to say to whomever you need to say it. Whenever you feel complete, simply imagine yourself going back through the door you entered. Take a few minutes to get back into the present moment and in connection with your body by following your breath. Afterwards, you might want to write down what happened during your meditation. Like with dreaming, I often imagine I will remember but the memory gets fuzzy fairly quickly.

Stream of Consciousness Writing:

This is a practice I learned from *The Artist's Way* by Julia Cameron. She calls it Morning Pages because it is best done in the morning. It is a lovely way to sweep out the cobwebs and set the tone for the day. I have found it to be a very simple but profound exercise, yielding surprises, delights and insights. With pen and paper in hand (as opposed to typing on a computer), you begin writing. Write about anything, or nothing. Writing, "I don't know what to write" ten times is a totally valid option. The point is to keep the pen moving, to keep the energy flowing, for three full (ideally 8 ½" x 11") pages. It may be tempting to stop if you don't think you know what to say. It may be tempting to censor, to edit, to judge yourself; this exercise is not about that. The goal is to create a safe space for your energy, thoughts and expression. Your relationship to expression and how it has been nurtured (or not) in the past will likely be revealed here. It might take a little time before you get the hang of it, but I encourage you to stick with it, it is a profound act of self-love to give yourself this time and attention.

"Yes, And" and Creation Writing:

There is a fun game I learned about in improv, and, in fact, people use it in all kinds of training and team-building exercises because it is so enlightening and so effective. It's called "Yes, and". It is played with two people, one of whom offers an idea. The other partner simply responds with "No." The first person offers another idea and is again met with a "No". They may repeat that dynamic a few more times. The two people are then invited to tune into what that experience feels like. What do they notice about having the energy of their offering go nowhere? This next time one partner offers a new idea and instead of rejecting the idea, the other partner enthusiastically says, "Yes, and..." and then proceeds to offer more to the idea, no matter how fanciful or ridiculous. For example, person A offers: "I'd like to take you on a picnic." Person B responds with "Yes, and we could take my car and a frisbee." Person A adds, "Yes, and we could stop for ice cream first."

The two partners go back and forth, "Yes, and", until the time is up, or until their faces hurt too much to go on from all of the smiling and laughing. Then they tune into what that experience was like. What does it feel like to have that level of possibility; to have that kind of collaboration; to have that kind of partnership and enthusiastic support with another?

Through my own writing exploration, I have discovered a kind of writing that I call "Creation Writing". It is a lot like doing the "Yes, and" exercise but instead of doing it with another you simply do it with yourself and instead of doing it verbally, it happens on the paper. It begins by finding an idea or thought that inspires you or is just something you would like to explore more. Without censoring, begin writing about it; get really descriptive and give a lot of detail. Which part of that is most alive? Which part feels the most fun or joyful? Follow that, write more about that, and help it grow. Follow the next bit of life in the flow, where will it take you? Follow the Yes! Again, like with Morning Pages, don't censor yourself, allow it all. Don't try to predict where it will go, just stay on the ride until you have reached the shining answer. You will recognize it when it happens. I have learned so much about myself, my desires and my dreams by allowing small ideas to flourish uncensored through Creation Writing.

Finding Your Focus:

The idea behind finding or crafting your focus is to have a written statement that reflects what your compass heading is at a particular point in time; rather like a personal mission statement but more short term and specific. Where do you want to put your attention lately? Is it on your physical health, your creativity, your relationship, your career, or someplace else? Whatever it is jot down what you would like to see as an end goal. "I'd like my body to be healthier", for example. Now, you get to fluff that up, amp it up, by adding more specifics to it. How would you like to feel in your body? How would you like your body to feel? Maybe your answer is "I'd like to feel strong". Well, how strong? What could you do with that strength? What are some colorful adjectives to include, or superlatives describing how you would like to experience it? Check in regularly to make sure it is still feeling authentic. Keep crafting until you get a focus statement that gives you goosebumps or makes you say, "Yes!" (It helps to phrase you focus in the present tense.) Ultimately you might get to a focus that sounds something like, "I am thrilled to be taking excellent care of my beloved body so that I am able to experience amazing and life-expanding adventures". This is only one potential direction, yours is likely to be completely different as only you know where you're headed.

Raising the Vibration

You have the power to effect change in your circle, and in the world at large, just by being your own best self. To me that is amazing, and, what joy, there is even more you can do to lift us all.

Light House Meditation:

Begin by using the Grounding Meditation from above. Once you feel present and connected to yourself, imagine you are standing on top of a mountain of your choosing or at the top of a lighthouse. Look at (or feel) the view all around you. Do you see or sense water, land, mountains? Next, imagine you are feeling one of these emotions: love, joy, peace or unconditional acceptance. Fill your whole being with the quality of that emotion and let it build to overflowing. Then imagine that emotion broadcasting out of your being. It might be coming from your heart, from your third eye between your eyebrows, or from your whole being, trust your intuition on this. Next imagine this energy is traveling as far beyond yourself as you wish. It could cover your town, your portion of the country or it could blanket the entire world or beyond. Feel that energy continue to flow until it comes to a natural stop. Sit quietly for a while longer, enjoying the reverberations throughout your body before moving on with your day. If you still feel too expanded when you are finished, read something small, drink some water or rub your arms or feet to help you come back to your everyday self.

Prayer:

Never underestimate the power of prayer. That's what many people say, and I agree. I pray all the time. Whenever I see anything that I am not able to directly help with I pray. I pull in patron saints; I pull in the big gun Archangels. I once heard that there are *unemployed angels* who are literally waiting to be called into duty. I call on them all the time. There is no downside to prayer. Ask for help, ask for assistance. You don't even need to believe that there is anyone out there, just releasing a request for help, will benefit you. Pray for yourself, pray for others, pray for the environment and the planet. I usually simply pray a generic and benign *love and light* prayer. I will randomly put out a prayer for a specific group: people who are struggling with substance abuse, for example, or people who are feeling afraid in that moment. My father had a prayer list that he kept in his shirt pocket so that he could add someone at a moment's notice. He would pray every morning for those on his list. I used to doubt that it did any good but now I believe that there is more support than we could possibly fathom and not one of those beings will ever get mad at us for asking for *too much*.

Embodying Your Vibe:

When you are trying to home in on what you are about, make a list of words which resonate with you. You can use a thesaurus to find synonyms for words that you already know you like and that way you can fine-tune them to something that really resonates. You can add to the list as you go through life and notice more words that describe who you are or words that make you feel the way you want to feel. You can eventually customize those lists. Which words comfort or calm you? Which words lift you up or make you want to get moving? Which words inspire you and help you dream bigger?

You can also (or instead) use pictures. Perhaps you respond more to a visual image. Photograph, tear out from a magazine, take a screenshot of any image you see that makes you feel any of the feelings you want to feel, expansive, aligned, or joyful, for example. You could keep these words or images in your journal, post them on the bathroom mirror, or tattoo one or more to remind yourself of the vibe or vibes that feel true to you.

Music is also an excellent way to curate your vibration. Having an Authentic Playlist with songs that connect you with your essence can elevate your day just by you hitting *play*.

And Then We All Get to Shine

ACKNOWLEDGEMENTS

I offer my love, appreciation and gratitude to the following, for their part in my becoming - you will never know the impact you have had:

To my Mom and Dad for giving me life, love and a warm, safe home.

To their ancestors for giving them life and for all of the good genes.

To my siblings for love, fun, friendship, support, and for offering me a reflection that has been helpful, sometimes challenging and mostly wonderful.

To Wayne for being my best friend, my mirror and my partner in life and growth.

To Carli for agreeing to be my first child, and for inspiring me with your adventurous spirit.

To Elaina for our deep talks and your never-ending warmth.

To Glenn for teaching me so much about authenticity. Authentic or die.

To my in-laws for welcoming me, cheering for me, and loving me.

To my friends and family of choice along the way for fun, for listening, for sharing your authentic selves with me and for accepting mine.

To these talented, loving, and wise practitioners, teachers and mentors, thank you for sharing your gifts with me; for seeing and believing in me; and for helping me to become my Authentic Self: Agnes Smith, Robin Masci, Ruth Berlin, Julie Hutslar, Barb Perusse, Terra McDonald, Hallie Owen, Brietta Leader and the Gypsy Divas, Cynthia Stamation, Paul Castro, Kyle Mercer, Caren Reiner, Mark Reiner, Michael Pinchera, Peter Mico, Michelle Kaminski, Erin Brandt and Anya Kalina.

To the Sandpoint Men's Group for helping to keep Wayne alive and for community, support, and love for me and for our family.

To the (now defunct) Integral Center and Robert MacNaughton and Michael Welp for teaching me the incredibly genuine art of Authentic Relating.

To the wonderful women (past and present) in the Wild Women Writers Group for holding space and for inspiring me with your fierce Authentic Selves.

To God/Goddess, the angels and saints, and my amazing Spiritual Support Squad for your unlimited love, support, protection, and guidance, and for every day I get to live in this world.

And Then We All Get to Shine

RECOMMENDED READING AND RESOURCES

The Artist's Way by Julia Cameron
The Vein of Gold by Julia Cameron
Nonviolent Communication: A Language of Compassion by Marshall Rosenberg
Astrology for the Soul by Jan Spiller
Pluto: The Evolutionary Journey of the Soul by Jeff Green
Radical Forgiveness by Colin Tipping
Patriarchy Stress Disorder by Valerie Rhein, PhD
Power vs Force by David R. Hawkins, M.D., PhD
The Body Keeps the Score by Bessel van der Kolk
The Road Less Traveled by M. Scott Peck, M.D.
The Diving Bell and the Butterfly by Jean-Dominique Bauby
The War of Art by Steven Pressfield
Breath: The New Science of a Lost Art by James Nestor
Do Nothing by Celeste Headlee
Daring Greatly by Brené Brown
Conflict = Energy: The Transformative Practice of Authentic Relating by Jason Diggs
In the Realm of Hungry Ghosts by Gabor Maté
Yoga: The Spirit and Practice of Moving into Stillness by Erich Schiffmann
Asana Pranayama Mudra Bandha by Swami Satyananda Saraswati
The Mask, the Mirror and the Illusion by Julie Hutslar
How to Be an Antiracist by Ibram X. Kendi
Between the World and Me by Ta-Nehisi Coates
America's Racial Karma: An Invitation to Heal by Larry Ward PhD
How to be You by Jeffrey Marsh
Little Weirds by Jenny Slate

Solfeggio Frequencies - https://mindeasy.com/the-9-solfeggio-frequencies-and-their-benefits/

Soul Piece Jewelry - https://www.facebook.com/soulpiecejewelry?mibextid=LQQJ4d

And the Music Played the Band video - https://www.youtube.com/watch?v=BDlreRnCYpg

The Moth Storytelling – www.themoth.org

Authentic Now Yoga – www.authenticnowyoga.com

Auroville - www.auroville.org

HeartMath - www.heartmath.com

BIBLIOGRAPHY

Cameron, Julia. (1992) The Artist's Way: A Spiritual Path to Higher Creativity. Jeremy P. Tarcher.

Cameron, Julia. (1997) The Vein of Gold: A Journey to Your Creative Heart. Jeremy P. Tarcher/Penguin.

Hawkins, Dr David R. (2012) Power vs Force: The Hidden Determinants of Human Behavior. Hay House.

Hutslar, Julie. (2014) The Mask, the Mirror and the Illusion: Awakening to the Knowledge of Who You Truly Are. Luminous Epinoia Press.

Pressfield, Steven. (2012) The War of Art: Break Through the Blocks and Win Your Inner Creative Battles. Black Irish Entertainment, LLC.

Pressfield, Steven. (2015) Do the Work. Black Irish Entertainment, LLC.

And Then We All Get to Shine

ABOUT THE AUTHOR

Jody Pignolet is a yoga instructor, writer, singer, dancer, parent and partner. She has been tracking her authenticity for most of her life, a quest that has brought her immense joy and peace. She combines her love of yoga, the present moment and authenticity to support others in embracing their Authentic Selves. A Midwestern girl by birth, she calls the Pacific Northwest home.

Made in the USA
Las Vegas, NV
27 March 2024